U.S. History Skillbook

**Practice and Application of
Historical Thinking Skills
for AP* U.S. History**

4th Edition

by Michael Henry, Ph.D.

SHERPALEARNING
GUIDING YOU TO EVEN GREATER HEIGHTS

Sherpa Learning is dedicated to helping high-achieving learners gain access to high-quality, skills-based instruction that is created, reviewed, and tested by teachers. To learn more about Sherpa Learning and our vision, or to learn about some of our upcoming projects, please visit us at **www.sherpalearning.com**.

Publisher/Editor: David Nazarian

Copy Editor: Christine DeFranco

Cartographer: Sal Esposito

Cover Design (4ᵗʰ Ed.): David Nazarian

* AP is a registered trademark of the College Board, which was not involved in the production of, and does not endorse, this product.

ISBN 978-1-948641-02-9

SHERPALEARNING
GUIDING YOU TO EVEN GREATER HEIGHTS

10 9 8 7 6 5 4 3 2

To the three women in my life:

    my wife Ann,

    my daughter Kimberly,

    and my granddaughter Gracie.

Table of Contents

Table of Contents

Content/Skills Overview

This book is designed differently than traditional AP U.S. History test-prep books. Whereas those texts focus on drilling you with content, this text focuses on improving your historical thinking and writing skills. In an Advanced Placement or Honors history course, you must do more than simply memorize facts, read a document, and regurgitate information on objective tests. You must become adept at applying advanced historical thinking skills, analyzing documents, and writing strong argumentative essays. The exercises in this book are designed to do just that.

The structure of the 4th EDITION has been carefully aligned to the curriculum framework of the redesigned AP U.S. History course and exam, including the revisions released in the summer of 2017. As you progress through the chapters in this book, you will be introduced to the two AP History Disciplinary Practices of **Analyzing Historical Evidence** and **Argument Development**. In addition, you will begin to master the four Reasoning Skills of **Contextualization, Comparison, Causation,** and **Continuity and Change over Time (C.C.O.T.).** Later chapters will build upon the skills introduced in earlier chapters toward the ultimate goal of writing full-length essay responses to Document-Based Question (DBQ) and Long Essay Question (LEQ) prompts.

The table provided below and on the next two pages is designed to give you an overview of how the content and skills are arranged throughout this text.

Unit	Chapter	Topic	Disciplinary Practice/ Reasoning Skill
1	1	Separating Fact from Opinion	Analyzing Evidence
	2	Identifying the Purpose of the Question	Argument Development
	3	Determining Status Quo vs. Change	Continuity and Change over Time (C.C.O.T.)

Content/Skills Overview

Unit	Chapter	Topic	Disciplinary Practice/ Reasoning Skill
2	**4**	Creating Categories for Understanding	Causation
	5	Using H.I.P.P.O. to Interpret Documents	Analyzing Evidence
	6	What the Prompt is Asking You to Do	Argument Development
3	**7**	Linking Cause and Effect	Causation
	8	Establishing the Credibility of Documents	Analyzing Evidence
	9	Making Inferences to Expand Meaning	Analyzing Evidence
	10	Contextualizing Events	Contextualization
	11	Analyzing Secondary Sources	Analyzing Evidence (Secondary Sources)
4	**12**	Using Graphs and Maps Effectively	Analyzing Evidence
	13	Establishing Point of View	Analyzing Evidence
	14	Using Documents in an Essay	Argument Development
	15	Using Contrasting Documents	Argument Development
	16	Developing a Thesis	Argument Development
	17	Contextualization and Chart Analysis	Contextualization

Unit	Chapter	Topic	Disciplinary Practice/ Reasoning Skill
5	18	Extending and Modifying a Thesis	Argument Development
	19	Cartoons and Contextualization	Argument Dev., Contextualization
	20	Comparing and Contrasting Historical Positions	Comparison
	21	Using Documents and Charts in an Essay	Analyzing Evidence, C.C.O.T., Contextualization
6	22	Recognizing Relevant Evidence	Analyzing Evidence
	23	Using Facts to Support a Thesis	Analyzing Evidence, Argument Dev.
	24	Using Documents and Cartoons in an Essay	Argument Dev., Contextualization
7	25	Bias and Point of View	Argument Dev.
	26	Interpreting Secondary Sources	Analyzing Evidence (Secondary Sources)
	27	Grouping Documents into Categories	Analyzing Evidence, Argument Dev., C.C.O.T.
	28	Creating an Introductory Paragraph	Argument Dev., Contextualization
	29	Writing a Concluding Paragraph	Argument Dev., Contextualization

Content/Skills Overview

Unit	Chapter	Topic	Disciplinary Practice/ Reasoning Skill
8	30	Prioritizing Facts in Planning an Essay	Analyzing Evidence, Argument Dev.
	31	Sequencing Evidence in an Essay	Analyzing Evidence, Argument Dev.
	32	Steps for Writing a DBQ Essay	ALL SIX
	33	Steps for Writing an LEQ Essay	ALL SIX
9	34	A Review of the Disciplinary Practices and Reasoning Skills	ALL SIX
	35	Writing a DBQ Essay	ALL SIX
	36	Writing an LEQ Essay	ALL SIX
	37	Understanding the DBQ and LEQ Rubrics	ALL SIX

Chronological Periods Overview

The Units of this book have been aligned to the nine Historical Periods outlined by the College Board® in the new AP U.S. History course framework. This will allow you to sync up the thinking and writing exercises in this book with the content you are covering in class. Or, if you prefer to dive into the development of skills later in the year, the exercises will serve as a review of materials covered earlier in the course.

Unit	Chapters	Historical Period
1	1-3	Period 1: 1491–1607
2	4-6	Period 2: 1607–1754
3	7-11	Period 3: 1754–1800
4	12-17	Period 4: 1800–1848
5	18-21	Period 5: 1844–1877
6	22-24	Period 6: 1865–1898
7	25-29	Period 7: 1890–1945
8	30-33	Period 8: 1945–1980
9	34-37	Period 9: 1980–Present

Introduction

For a student, an AP course in United States History offers a daunting challenge: how to master an entire year's work in American history and demonstrate proficiency of that knowledge on an examination at the end of the course. This book is designed to make that task easier by providing a complement to your existing text book. While it is an addendum to your study of American history, the volume serves as more than a test preparation manual. The text will enhance your thinking and writing abilities in ways that you will find useful in other high school courses, in college, and beyond.

The main focus of the book is to develop your document analysis and writing proficiencies by providing activities in preparation for composing Document-Based Questions (DBQs) and Long Essay Questions (LEQs). The text is organized with the early chapters addressing basic skills, such as the focus of a prompt, and the later material becoming increasingly complex as you move deeper into the book. Thus, by the last unit, you will be ready to write full-length, high-scoring DBQ and LEQ essays.

The book is constructed around the two AP History Disciplinary Practices and the four Reasoning Skills that comprise the redesigned AP U.S. History curriculum introduced in the summer of 2017. These skills form the organizational core of the text, and the various activities will help you analyze evidence, make comparisons, establish causation, construct effective arguments, deal with change over time, and interpret historical documents. Collectively these activities define critical inquiry, which is a process that will serve you well in your AP classes and throughout your high school and college career.

The text breaks these thinking activities into their component parts. For example, when you work on analyzing evidence, you will study several facets of the skill, such as separating fact from opinion and prioritizing and sequencing facts within your essay. By developing these "habits of the mind," you will expand your abilities as a writer and thinker.

The book has several instructional applications. It can serve in your classroom as a companion to the textbook. With this arrangement, you can build thinking, writing, and analytical skills as you progress through the nine time periods that make up the redesigned curriculum. The book can also serve as a separate writing and skill tutorial, helping you to prepare on your own for writing responses to DBQ and LEQ prompts.

You may want to form study groups and work through the materials as the final exam or end-of-course exam approaches. For an individual student, the book is useful in reinforcing essay writing and primary source analytical skills. With its easy-to-use format, you will find it to be an effective tool when preparing essays and analyzing documents.

I hope that this book proves to be a valuable tool in your quest to master the AP U.S. History curriculum this year, culminating with a 5 on the exam in May. Good luck!

Michael Henry

Additional Resources Available Online

https://www.sherpalearning.com/skillbook

Detailed Summaries of each of the nine Historical Periods

Discussion Questions

Blank Worksheet Templates:
- H.I.P.P.O. (Document Analysis)
- D.A.I.L.Y. (Cartoon Analysis)
- P.O.W.S. (Document Credibility)
- The 5 Ts (Chart Analysis)
- Short-Answer Response Sheets
- DBQ & LEQ Planners
- DBQ & LEQ Rubric Guides

Glossary of Period Highlights and Key Terms

Visual Source Exercises:
- Maps
- Charts & Graphs
- Political Cartoons
- Paintings & Illustrations
- Photographs

Sample Responses to some of the essay prompts in this text

Submit your own essays to have them scored by the author, Mike Henry!

Also, each essay you submit offers you a chance to win stuff. See our website for more info.

Scan the QR Code to link directly to the companion website on your mobile device.

If you're using a desktop or laptop, simply point your browser to the URL shown above.

Unit 1

The Atlantic World

"Coronado sets out to the north"
— oil painting by Frederic Remington

Period 1: 1491–1607

Period Summary

The Atlantic World is a historical construct that defines how four landmasses that border the Atlantic Ocean—Africa, Europe, North America, and South America (including the Caribbean and Central America)—interacted and influenced each other from the 1420s until the middle of the 17th century. It serves as a means for examining European contact as well as exploration and settlement in Africa and in the Western Hemisphere. The rise of the Atlantic World created new global economies and social systems that expanded markets, redistributed wealth, and transformed cultures in the four regions.

All European countries had difficulty populating their colonies. Life was hard and dangerous. Europeans quickly enslaved the native peoples and Africans to solve their labor problems. Although France attempted to coexist with the Indians, England and Spain took the natives' land and destroyed their way of life. European expansion laid the foundation of the modern Atlantic World as it destroyed native peoples and cultures in its wake.

Ideas for Discussion

1. What factors prompted Portugal and Spain to expand in the 15th and 16th centuries?

2. Why did the Europeans have an interest in Africa in the late 15th century?

3. How was slavery a different institution in Africa, Europe, and the Western Hemisphere?

4. In what ways was Christopher Columbus a hero and a villain?

5. Who benefited most/least from the Columbian Exchange?

6. What role did religion play in shaping the Atlantic World?

Extend Your Understanding

For a complete review of Period 1: 1491–1607 and more Ideas for Discussion, scan the code or go to
www.sherpalearning.com/skillbook/review/unit-1

Separating Fact from Opinion

The ability to sort and use evidence is the life blood of historical investigation. All generalizations, hypotheses, and arguments must be based on facts. It is essential that you have a clear realization of what *is*

and *is not* sound factual evidence in history. Only with this fundamental understanding, can you make supportable inferences and draw reasoned conclusions about historical events and phenomena.

At its most basic level, this skill is about making a distinction between appropriate and inappropriate evidence. To begin making that distinction, you must first be able to distinguish between fact and opinion. Too often students depend on personal beliefs as their only support for a historical event. Many might mistakenly accept their own opinion as a self-evident truth that they consider to be both accurate and indisputable. As you develop a better understanding of the difference between fact and opinion, you'll train your mind to recognize alternative points of view and strengthen your ability to evaluate evidence.

By using factual information rather than opinions in an answer, you are adding specificity to your argument. **Specificity adds credibility**—it makes your response more convincing. A fact is something that is known with certainty. In other words, it really happened and can be proven or documented. Although the message it conveys may be subject to interpretation, the data or information itself can always be authenticated . By contrast, an opinion is something that someone *thinks* is true. It often reflects a point of view or bias held by a person, and it cannot be authenticated or confirmed. Essentially, there is no proof to support the claim. Opinions are always debatable and may contain words that indicate a judgment is being made, such as *bad, good, great, beautiful, most, least,* and so on.

There are several sections in this book that deal with using relevant evidence as specific, provable information in your written responses. In this first lesson, you'll practice recognizing facts and opinions in a variety of arguments. Later, in Chapters 22, 23, 30, and 31, there will be further discussions about using facts rather than generalizations and opinions to effectively support written arguments.

Practicing the Skill

Directions: Look at the prompt below about the Atlantic World and determine which of the three answers that follow are factual and verifiable, and which are opinions or points of view.

Example Prompt: *What role did religion play in shaping the Atlantic World?*

Answer 1 — Religion played an important role in the Atlantic World because native religions were superstitious rather than spiritual and had to be changed.

Answer 2 — Religion played an important role in the Atlantic World as priests and missionaries converted one million Indians to Catholicism.

Answer 3 — Religion played an important role in the Atlantic World when Pope Alexander VI gave his blessing to Spanish and Portuguese exploration and conquest.

Let's see how you did. Answer 1 is an opinion. Native American religions were spiritual in nature. Answer 2 is a fact. This statement can be verified. Answer 3 is an opinion. The pope's blessing had no effect on Dutch, French, or British exploration and conquest.

Applying the Skill

Directions: Study the exercise questions that follow. Determine which of the answers are factual and verifiable, and which of the answers are opinions or points of view. Explain your reasoning for labeling each answer as either fact or opinion.

Exercise Prompt 1: *Why were the Inca and Aztec unable to defend their civilization from conquest by the conquistadors?*

Answer 1 The Inca and the Aztec faced internal divisions that kept them from defeating the Spanish.

Answer 2 The Inca and the Aztec were unable to defend their way of life because the Spanish superior culture appealed to many of their subjects.

Answer 3 The Inca and the Aztec were outsmarted by the Spanish and manipulated into surrender.

Exercise Prompt 2: *Why did the Europeans have an interest in Africa in the late 15th century?*

Answer 1 Africans were backward people unable to defend their valuable natural resources.

Answer 2 Africans did not care about their fellow Africans and allowed them to be easily enslaved by the Europeans.

Answer 3 Africa was an attractive source of trade goods, including slave labor, which Europeans wanted.

Identifying the Purpose of the Question

Advanced Placement classes are well known for the emphasis—and expectations—they place on writing. The skill that you need to demonstrate most in your various essay answers is that of historical argumentation. The first step to mastering this skill is to learn to identify the purpose of the question you've been asked to answer. If you begin by identifying the type of prompt, then you will be able to determine what you are required to do to answer the question successfully.

> **DISCIPLINARY PRACTICE**
> - **Argument Development**

The four reasoning skills that are highlighted in the AP U.S. History curriculum are **Continuity and Change over Time, Causation, Comparison,** and **Contextualization**. While Contextualization is a reasoning skill that is evaluated in the course and on the examination, it will not appear as a stand-alone prompt on the exam. In this section, however, examples of possible contextualization questions are included. This will introduce the idea and help you to see how providing perspective and background in your essay can improve it and enrich it.

There are several types of essay prompts that you are likely to encounter on tests and quizzes for this course, and on the exam in May. Review the common types of essay prompts that follow, and closely examine the examples for each.

Continuity and Change over Time:

Almost all essays have an element of change in them, but some will specifically ask you to account for change within a defined period of time, and to identify and explain the factors that brought about the transformation.

> **Example Prompt 1:** *Between 1492 and 1540, how and why did Spain alter its colonial system of administration?*

Another type of Continuity and Change over Time essay is one that asks you to account for both change and continuity stemming from or promoted by an event or series of events.

> **Example Prompt 2:** *Evaluate the extent to which economic developments in North and South America contributed to maintaining continuity, as well as fostering change, in European life from 1492–1600.*

Causation:

This type of prompt requires you to identify causes of events and to LINK them to historical outcomes. You must consider both short- and long-term cause-and-effect relationships with this type of prompt and make sure to organize the causes in terms of relative importance.

> **Example Prompt 3:** *How did the need for labor in the Western Hemisphere transform trade relations in the Atlantic World?*

Comparison:

These essays often involve an analysis of similarities and differences between events and topics. When you encounter this type of prompt, you should make sure you analyze both the pros and cons of the issues. Remember, when you draw contrasts between topics, you are also comparing them.

> **Example Prompt 4:** *Compare and contrast the Spanish and British motives for colonization from 1492–1607.*

Contextualization:

We will expand on Contextualization and its relevance in Chapters 10 and 17, but in this section, we will give some examples of prompts that would require its development. As you develop your written arguments, it is important to put events into their time and place. In this way, you will help to establish a perspective and suggest possible influences to the topic under analysis.

> **Example Prompt 5:** *How did developments in Europe in the decades before 1492 set the stage for Spain's exploration of the Western Hemisphere?*

Applying the Skill

Directions: Develop a prompt for each of the following essay types, using the suggested subjects. Write your prompts in your notebook. When you have finished, discuss your work with the class.

1. A comparison prompt about Spanish and English policies toward Native American peoples.

2. A causation prompt about the impact of slavery on the Atlantic World.

3. A change-over-time prompt about French internal politics and the desire for North American colonies.

4. A contextualization prompt about the motivation and background of the Spanish conquistadors.

Determining
Status Quo vs. Change

In the previous lesson concerning types of prompts likely to appear in the course curriculum and on the exam, you were introduced to the concept of addressing continuity and change over time. In this section, we'll examine this historical reasoning skill in greater detail.

REASONING SKILL

- **Continuity and Change over Time**

The process of accounting for change over time often manifests itself in two ways:

1. One form of change over time asks you to consider how events or processes evolved in an era and to analyze the causes of the transformation. With this type of problem, you must look carefully at the dates that are to be examined. These dates should establish the historical significance of the period under investigation. They should not be randomly selected because they serve a purpose and often indicate the theme that should be addressed in your answer. In addition, you must always deal with the *entire period* and make certain that all aspects of the problem are considered. To deal with only *some* developments in a time-frame is an inadequate response.

2. A second iteration of change over time seems to say, "The more things change, the more they stay the same." In other words, this type of prompt will require you to explain how events or processes both reinforced the status quo and, yet still, contributed to new ideas, relationships, and developments. Your job, in answering

this type of prompt, is to account for how events and processes represented a conserving *and* a transformational element in a time period. You're not being asked to choose between continuity and change; you are required to address both. That means you will have to accept small amounts of either conservation or evolution in your response. Also, you may find that certain topics lend themselves to an imbalance between how much actually remained the same, versus how much changed.

Practicing the Skill

PART 1

Directions: Briefly explain how the following topics changed European society from 1440–1500.

Topic 1: *Geographic understandings of the world and the search for pathways to Asia*

Suggested Responses

Possible elements of change could include:

- Prince Henry's influence in developing geographic tools and shipbuilding that resulted in Portugal's exploration of Africa

- By mid-15th century, shippers and explorers clear that the world was round

- Portuguese trading posts established on coasts of Africa, India, and China

- Columbus's idea of opening new trade routes to Asia by sailing west across ocean; 1492, Columbus's voyage to Bahamas

Topic 2: *The influx of gold and silver from Western Hemisphere into Europe*

Suggested Responses

Possible elements of change could include:

- Spanish plundering of gold and silver vastly expanded amount of species in circulation
- Benefited only a few wealthy individuals
- Caused great inflation in Europe
- Lowered the standard of living for many
- Rising prices depressed wages by more than 50%

PART 2

Directions: Read the prompt and then complete the chart below by brainstorming evidence of continuity and change.

Example Prompt: *To what extent did the Protestant Reformation contribute to maintaining continuity as well as foster change in European societies from 1517–1607?*

Continuity	Change
• Most of Europe remained Catholic • Pope remained a powerful political figure • Europeans continued to struggle over religion • Catholic church remained a powerful political and economic force	• Rise of dissent over Catholicism • Anglican Church established in England • Rise of French Huguenots • Rise of Calvinism • Many new religions grew up (Lutherans)

Applying the Skill

PART 1

Directions: Briefly explain how the following topics changed the exploration of the Western Hemisphere from 1440–1607.

Topic 1: *The development of the African slave trade*

Topic 2: *The introduction of sugar and maize into people's diets*

PART 2

Directions: Read the prompt, and then complete the chart below in your notebook.

Example Prompt: *To what extent did Native American's encounters with Europeans contribute to maintaining continuity as well as foster change in Native American's daily lives from 1492–1607?*

Continuity	Change

Unit 2
The Colonial Period

"Anne Hutchinson on Trial"
— by Edwin Austin Abbey, 1901

Period 2: 1607–1754

Period Summary

At the beginning of the 17th century, England was in turmoil. A population explosion and economic upheaval left many people rootless and impoverished. Religious struggles between the Anglican Church and other religious groups created a spiritual malaise as well. The newly opened areas of the Western Hemisphere beckoned to many people as a refuge from the difficulties at home. After several failed attempts, a permanent colony was established at Jamestown, Virginia, in the spring of 1607.

Despite their differences, by 1770 the colonies had developed a nascent American identity. The focus and form of this new feeling was still not clear, but as Britain sought to end its salutary neglect of the colonies, its manifestation became more concrete and explosive.

Ideas for Discussion

1. In the early 17th century, what conditions in England "pushed" people towards the North American colonies?

2. What hardship did the early colonists in British North America face? How did these challenges shape the character of the people?

3. Why was there a labor shortage in the colonies? How did the English try to solve it?

4. What economic activities developed in the various regions? Compare and contrast economic life in New England, mid-Atlantic, and Chesapeake colonies.

5. How did religious beliefs affect the development of the colonies from 1607 to 1763?

6. Why did the slave system evolve in the middle of the 17th century?

Extend Your Understanding

For a complete review of Period 2: 1607–1754 and more Ideas for Discussion, scan the code or go to
www.sherpalearning.com/skillbook/review/unit-2

Creating Categories for Understanding

The skill of establishing causation in history requires you to connect events or a series of events to new outcomes, developments, and actions. One of the most basic means to establish these connections

is to identify, analyze, and evaluate relationships by creating categories of facts. Grouping information into categories with similar characteristics establishes meaning and is foundational in developing the skill of historical causation. Too often you learn information in isolation, with little thought to how events are connected to each other, and have influenced larger historical developments. You may learn many facts, but unless you go beyond memorization by grouping them into categories, you may fail to "see the forest for the trees." Categorization is a stepping-stone to establishing causation and developing generalizations and hypotheses. Practicing the skill of developing categories will be a crucial first step in establishing historical causation.

Practicing the Skill

Directions: Read the following example prompt, and then follow along as a relevant piece of historical evidence is categorized for a response.

> **Example Prompt:** *How did religious beliefs affect the development of the colonies from 1607–1754?*

Consider the Act of Toleration and decide which of the following three categories the Act best fits:

(A) Promoted Religious Diversity

(B) Represented Established Religion

(C) Directly Challenged Religious Practices

The best answer is (A). The Act of Toleration gave religious freedom to all Christian groups in Maryland, and would best fit into the category of "Promoted Religious Diversity."

Applying the Skill

Directions: Read the following list of terms from this historical period (Period 2: 1607–1754) and, in your notebook, place each of them into one of the following three categories:

(A) Promoted Religious Diversity

(B) Represented Established Religion

(C) Directly Challenged Religious Practices

1.	Act of Toleration	**6.**	Anglican Church
2.	Anne Hutchinson	**7.**	William Penn
3.	Jonathan Edwards	**8.**	Halfway Covenant
4.	Quakers	**9.**	Roger Williams
5.	First Great Awakening	**10.**	Congregational Church

Be prepared to defend each of your category choices. Could some of the people/events fit in to more than one category? After you have agreed on the placements, look at the original question and discuss it with your classmates.

Using H.I.P.P.O. to Interpret Documents

Another critical skill for success in the AP U.S. History course, and ultimately on the exam, is interpreting primary sources by analyzing their content, evaluating their point of view, and establishing their meaning. You must be able to deal with diverse historical interpretations found not only in secondary sources, but in primary source documents as well. This has become especially important since the release of the redesigned AP U.S. History course and exam.

The new Document-Based Question (DBQ) calls on you to account for the historical context, the intended audience, the point of view, and/or the purpose of at least three sources in the question. Then, after you have deconstructed the document, you are expected to organize its components and incorporate them into your argument. To accomplish this, you would greatly benefit by having a consistent, systematic tool to use when interpreting sources.

Thankfully, such a device exists and is easy to remember—**H.I.P.P.O.** will help you unlock and use the meaning of a document!

★ **H.I.P.P.O.**

H. **H**istorical Context—What was the time or setting?

I. **I**ntended Audience—Where was the message directed?

P. **P**oint of View—What was the author's message?

P. **P**urpose—Why was it written? What did it hope
       to accomplish?

O. **O**rganize/Use—How will this source advance my
       thesis/argument?

In this section, we will focus on the first four parts of the tool (**H.I.P.P.**). We will address the **O** (Organize/Use) piece of the strategy in Chapter 14.

Practicing the Skill

Directions: Read the sample document below. After reading this letter, discuss the suggested answers to the first four parts of the **H.I.P.P.O.** strategy shown below.

Document 1

Source: William Penn to the Delaware Indian Chiefs, 1681

My friends, there is one great God and power that has made the world and all things. This great God has written his law in our hearts by which we are taught to love, help, and to do good to one another. Now this great God has been pleased to make me concerned in your part of the world. The king of the country where I live has given unto me a great province, but I desire to enjoy it with your love and consent, that we may always live together as neighbors and friends. … I have great love and regard towards you and I desire to gain your love and friendship by a kind, and peaceable life…

Sample Application of H.I.P.P.O.:

Historical Context: 1681 when Pennsylvania was founded by Quakers. Their leader, William Penn, hoped to share the land peacefully with the Native Americans.

Intended Audience: The Delaware Indian Chiefs AND the settlers of Pennsylvania.

Point of View: A call for peace, cooperation, and trust between Quakers and Native Americans.

Purpose: To reassure the Native Americans and to set a philosophical tone for dealing with the indigenous peoples of Pennsylvania.

Document 2

Source: Roger Williams, from *The Bloudy Tenent of Persecution*, 1644

God requireth not an uniformity of religion to be enacted and enforced by any civil state; …enforced uniformity…is the greatest occasion of civil war, ravishing of conscience, persecution of Christ Jesus in his servants, and of hypocrisy and destruction of millions of souls. …the Church of Christ does not use the arm of secular power to compel men to the true profession of truth, for this is done with spiritual weapons, whereby Christians are to be exhorted, not compelled.

Sample Application of H.I.P.P.O.:

Historical Context: Roger Williams, a religious dissenter, was exiled from Massachusetts Bay in 1635. He was the founder of Providence (Rhode Island).

Intended Audience: The people of Providence and others in New England who sought more religious freedom.

Point of View: Williams advocated religious diversity and freedom. He called for religious separation of church (civil state) and state (government).

Purpose: To lay out the religious philosophy of Providence, and call attention to the differences between Williams' colony and Massachusetts Bay.

Applying the Skill

Directions: Below you will find two more primary documents. Use the first four parts of **H.I.P.P.O.** to analyze the source, and then discuss the various elements as a class.

Document 3

Source: *Fundamental Orders of Connecticut*, **January 14, 1639**

We the inhabitants and residents of Windsor, Hartford and Wethersfield. ...well knowing where a people are gathered together the word of God requires that to maintain the peace and union of such a people there should be an orderly and decent government established according to God...

1. It is ordered, sentenced and decreed that there shall be yearly two general assemblies or courts ...

4. It is ordered that no person be chosen governor above once in two years, and that the governor be always a member of some approved congregation.

Document 4

Source: Eliza Lucas, *Journal and Letters,* **1742**

Now, dear brother, I will obey your command and give you a short description of the part of the world in which I now live. South Carolina is a vast region near the sea. Most of the settled part is flat ... South Carolina is filled with fine navigable rivers and great forests of fine timber. The soil in general is fertile. There are few European or American fruits or grains that cannot be grown here...

The people in general are hospitable and honest. The better sort of people are polite and gentle. The poorest sort are the laziest people in the world. Otherwise they would never be poor and wretched in a land as rich as this.

What the Prompt is Asking You to Do

In Chapter 2, we introduced the concept of historical argumentation when dealing with different types of Long Essay Question (LEQ) prompts. In this chapter, we will expand this skill by examining what a prompt asks you to do. When responding to an LEQ prompt, it is

DISCIPLINARY PRACTICE
- **Argument Development**

critical that you write on the correct topic and develop your response using the proper thinking skill. By writing an exceptional response to the wrong question, you will damage your performance both in your class and on the Advanced Placement examination. This is a very common mistake among students, but the good news is that it can be easily avoided! By simply asking yourself the following three questions, you will insure that your response correctly addresses the three major components of a prompt:

1. What time period should I write about?
2. What am I to do with the question?
3. What content is appropriate to use in answering the question?

Time Period

The time period may be stated outright in the question. If it is not, you must infer the proper time period from the details provided.

What to Do

With the redesigned curriculum, there are certain key phases that you should look for in an essay prompt. These phrases will help you to identify the proper historical thinking skill you should be using to develop your response to the prompt. Take a look at the following table of key phrases and their corresponding essay types.

Key Phrase	Essay Type
"…contributed to maintaining continuity as well as foster change…"	Continuity and Change over Time
"Evaluate the extent to which _____ impacted, influenced, caused, etc…."	Causation
"Compare and contrast…"	Comparison
"How did the developments before…" "Evaluate the background to…" "Evaluate the events that maintained continuity of…"	Contextualization*

*While it is unlikely a prompt will deal exclusively with the Reasoning Skill of Contextualization, it is an important factor to understand and include as you write your essay.

Content Areas

These are the most common content areas that essay questions may ask you to draw from as you support your argument.

Political—dealing with governmental issues, voting, parties, legislative action, and partisan affairs

Diplomatic—dealing with relations between the United States and other countries

Economic—dealing with financial issues, income, money, business activities, production, and distribution of goods and services

Social—dealing with people living together and their relationships with others in recreational, educational, and communal settings

Cultural—dealing with works of art and literature and their expressions of interests, skills, and dispositions of a time period

Intellectual—dealing with ideas, thoughts, understandings, and reasoning

Practicing the Skill

Directions: Examine the following prompt, and then attempt to answer the three questions. Next, compare your answers to the suggested answers that follow to make sure you understand the process of identifying the key parts of an essay.

> **Example Prompt:** *To what extent did the ideas of the Enlightenment impact the growth of democracy in British North America?*

(1) What time period should I write about?

(2) What am I to do with the question?

(3) What content is appropriate to use in answering the question?

Suggested Answers:

Time Period: 1607–1754

What to Do: Write a causation essay in which you connect the ideas of the Enlightenment to colonial, democratic practices, and ideals.

Content: political, intellectual, social aspects of the Enlightenment and their development in colonial American society

Applying the Skill

Directions: Read the prompt below and answer the three questions in your notebook. Then, discuss your response with your study group or with the entire class.

Exercise Prompt: *Compare and contrast the economic and social development of the colonies of Virginia and Massachusetts from 1607–1641.*

(1) What time period should I write about?

(2) What am I to do with the question?

(3) What content is appropriate to use in answering the question?

Unit 3

The Revolution & the New Nation

"The Spirit of '76"
— oil painting by A. M. Willard, 1876

Period 3: 1754–1800

Period Summary

At the conclusion of the Seven Years War, Great Britain dominated North America. In addition, the American colonists seemed content in the British imperial system. Mercantilism rested lightly on them as they enjoyed a strong measure of home rule. George III and Parliament controlled external matters, but the colonial assemblies made many local decisions.

Yet significant trouble began in 1764 when Parliament began passing a series of taxes—the most controversial of which was the Stamp Act. The colonists reacted strongly and the act was repealed in 1765. Nevertheless, the colonists became rebellious after a series of missteps by the British. In, 1773, the final crisis arrived with the Boston Tea Party. Responding to the Coercive Acts, the First and Second Continental Congresses met in Philadelphia where they petitioned the king, called for boycotts of British goods, organized an army, and finally issued the Declaration of Independence.

The Revolutionary war raged for seven years, but after the battle of Saratoga when France signed a treaty with the colonists, British efforts to subdue the colonials were doomed. After another British defeat at Yorktown in 1781, the British sought peace, and granted the colonies their independence in 1783. As they snapped the political bonds with England, the colonials constructed a new government to replace the monarchy. The product of this effort, the Articles of Confederation, was written in 1777 and ratified in 1781. Yet weaknesses gave rise to a call for a stronger central government that was instituted by the adoption of the Constitution and implemented in the first presidential administration under George Washington and John Adams.

Ideas for Discussion

1. How could one argue that the Americans did not win their independence, but rather that the British lost the colonies?

2. In what ways was the Revolution revolutionary? In what ways was it not?

Extend Your Understanding

For a complete review of Period 3: 1754–1800 and more Ideas for Discussion, scan the code or go to **www.sherpalearning.com/skillbook/review/unit-3**

Linking Cause and Effect

In Chapter 4, we began to examine the concept and skill of historical causation. In this section, we will expand upon that concept by establishing direct linkage between causes and effects. As with other thinking skills,

REASONING SKILL
• Causation

when you analyze and evaluate how one action impacted another event or development, you create and deepen your understanding of historical relationships. When you couple causes with their consequences, you are able to construct both short-term and long-term connections that help establish broader trends, generalizations, and themes that may not be apparent from the study of individual—and seemingly unrelated—facts. This ability to link causes to effects keeps history from becoming a mere litany of people, dates, and policies learned in isolation without any perception of their larger significance.

Practicing the Skill

Directions: To practice this skill, begin by analyzing the example prompt on the following page. Next, take a look at the suggested action (cause) below the prompt and brainstorm the relevant effects. Compare your answers to the suggested answers that follow.

> **Example Prompt:** *What single action between 1763 and 1776 was most damaging to British-colonial relations? Defend your choice.*

Cause: Seven Years War

Effects:

Suggested Answers:

Effects: Gave England a vast empire

Doubled the size of British debt

Created tension between Britain and colonies

Eliminated the French threat in North America

Applying the Skill

Directions: Continuing with the example prompt shown above, examine and consider the eight actions listed below. In your notebook, make a list of the effects each one had on British-colonial relations. After completing the list, decide which action was the most damaging in causing the rupture between England and its colonies. Be prepared to defend your choice.

1. **Cause:** Townshend Acts
    Effects?

2. **Cause:** Coercive Acts
    Effects?

3. **Cause:** Sugar Act

   Effects?

4. **Cause:** Boston Massacre

   Effects?

5. **Cause:** Stamp Act

   Effects?

6. **Cause:** Salutary Neglect

   Effects?

7. **Cause:** Stamp Act Congress

   Effects?

8. **Cause:** Boston Tea Party

   Effects?

Conclusion:

What was the most damaging action? Why?

Chapter
8

Establishing the Credibility of Documents

In Chapter 5, we discussed aspects of analyzing evidence by using the H.I.P.P.O. strategy. In this chapter, we will dig deeper into that process by evaluating the credibility of documents. In appraising multiple sources

DISCIPLINARY PRACTICE

• Analyzing Evidence

in general, and those found on the redesigned DBQ specifically, you must be able to accurately assess their credibility. You must determine whether they corroborate or contradict one another. And in this process, you must determine which document provides the soundest information about an event, incident, or phenomenon. In other words, you must evaluate the evidence in terms of its believability. This can be accomplished by establishing the historical context, intended audience, point of view, and purpose of the author in the document—**H.I.P.P.**!

Below are some questions that will help you assign credibility to a source and/or an author:

1. **Is the source a primary or secondary one?**

   A primary document is a first-hand account of an event. Examples of primary sources are letters, speeches, court rulings, and newspaper articles. A secondary source is written by someone who acquired the information second-hand and at a later date; they were not actually present at the event. An example of a secondary source is your history textbook. Primary sources are usually given greater weight than secondary sources, though not as a rule.

2. **Was the document produced at the time the event occurred?**

   Some primary sources, such as newspaper articles, journals, and diaries, are eyewitness accounts, but may have been written many years after the event. Always look for the date of the source, and where possible, expand your assessment by establishing the broader historical context of the document.

3. **What do you know about the writer?**

   Did they have a vested interest in the event that would color their perspective? Was there a bias or hidden agenda that might have affected the author's point of view/purpose when creating the source? Also, were they trying to sway a particular audience with their argument? For example, were they slaveholders defending the institution? Or did they command the ship that torpedoed the passenger liner?

4. **Was the writer in a position to know what happened?**

   Were they actually present at the battlefront or on the bow of the ship? Did their position influence their perspective and interpretation of what happened? Again the answers to these questions help establish point of view, purpose, and audience. The bottom line: could they give an accurate, unbiased account?

For the DBQ on the redesigned exam, you must deal with context, intended audience, point of view, and purpose. Since this is a timed essay, you must assess these components quickly in order to weigh the credibility of the various sources. For example, both William Lloyd Garrison and George Fitzhugh were first-hand observers of slavery, but they held diametrically opposing views, and wrote to very different audiences about the contextual nature of servitude in America. All these factors must be considered when deciding which man most accurately described the institution of slavery. To evaluate the credibility of sources, you must address the questions shown above. An efficient way to do this is with **P.O.W.S.**!

★ **P.O.W.S.**

When you come across a source, determine the following:

P. **Primary** or secondary source?

O. **Occasion** of the source—When was it produced? What else was happening? (Context)

W. **Writer's** agenda—Did he/she have a vested interest? (Point of view/Purpose/Audience)

S. **Standing** of the author—Could he/she really know? (Point of View/Purpose/Audience)

Practicing the Skill

Directions: Read the document below and use **P.O.W.S.** to interpret its credibility. When you've finished, compare your responses to the suggested answers that follow to evaluate your understanding of the process for determining credibility.

Document 1

Source: Thomas Fessenden, a colonial onlooker at Lexington, April 23, 1775

I, Thomas Fessenden, of lawful age, testify and declare, that being in a pasture near the meeting house at said Lexington, on Wednesday, last, at about half an hour before sunrise, ... I saw three officers on horseback advance to the front of said Regulars, when one of them being within six rods of the said Militia, cried out, "Disperse, you rebels, immediately;" on which he brandished his sword over his head three times; meanwhile, the second officer, who was about two rods behind him, fired a pistol pointed at the Militia, and the Regulars kept huzzaing till he had finished brandishing his sword.

Primary or secondary source?

Occasion of the source? (Context)

Writer's agenda? (Point of View/Purpose/Audience)

Standing of the author? (Point of View/Purpose/Audience)

Suggested Answers:

P. It is a primary source—a first-hand account.

O. It was written within a matter of days after the battle. The larger context was that for months the people of Massachusetts had been in conflict with the British because of the Coercive Acts growing out of the Boston Tea Party of December 1773.

W. He was a colonial partisan. He could harbor an anti-British point of view and his purpose might be to make the British appear to be the aggressors.

S. He was at the scene and could report on the event. His standing, however, as a resident of Lexington might make his fellow neighbors—who believed themselves victims of British oppression— his intended audience.

Applying the Skill

Directions: Below are two sets of documents about the battle of Lexington and Concord on April 19, 1775, and about the causes of the American Revolution. Read both sets of documents and use **P.O.W. S.** to interpret their credibility. Select one document from each set that is most believable. In your notebook, write a short rationale explaining why you made your selection.

SET 1: WHO FIRED FIRST?

Document 1

Use Document 1 (Fessenden) on p. 32.

Document 2

> **Source: Ensign Jeremy Lister, British officer, writing in 1832**
>
> However the best of my recollection about 4 oClock in the Morning being the 19th of April 5 front Compys [sic] was ordered to Load which we did, about half an hour after we found that precaution had been necessary, … it was Lexington when we saw one of their Compys [sic] drawn up in regular order Major Pitcairn of the Marines second in command call'd [sic] to them to disperse, but their not seeming willing he desired us to mind our space which we did when they gave us a fire then run off to get behind a wall.

Conclusion:

Which is the better source? Why?

SET 2: WHAT CAUSED THE REVOLUTION?

Document 3

> **Source: John R. Alden, *The American Revolution, 1775–1783* (written in 1954)**
>
> In the winter of 1774–75 the British government learned that America had become a powder keg. Blame for this situation must be attributed in far larger measure to the inadequacies of George III and British politicians than to the activities of the radical leadership in America. … Had the new policy been firmly and steadily pushed in the Stamp Act crisis, it is barely possible that American resistance might have been peacefully overcome. But wiser by far than a consistent course of coercion would have been the abandoning of the effort to turn back the colonial clock. An American policy to be based upon recognition of the maturity of the colonies and of their value to the mother country, together with an attitude of goodwill, might have postponed indefinitely the era of American independence… .

Document 4

Source: John Dickinson, *Letters from a Farmer in Pennsylvania*, 1767

The parliament unquestionably possesses a legal authority to regulate the trade of Great Britain, and all her colonies. Such an authority is essential to the relation between a mother country and her colonies.... This power is lodged in the parliament; and we are as much dependent on Great Britain, as a perfectly free people can be on another.

I have looked over every statute relating to these colonies, from their first settlement to this time; and I find every one of them founded on this principle, till the Stamp Act administration. All before, are calculated to regulate trade.... Thus the King by his judges in his courts of justice, imposes fines which all together amount to a very considerable sum, ... But this is merely a consequence arising from restrictions the British parliament till the period above mentioned, think of imposing duties in America fore THE PURPOSE OF RAISING A REVENUE ... that is, to raise money upon us without our consent.

Conclusion:

Which is the better source? Why?

Making Inferences to Expand Meaning

Earlier in the book, the focus was on determining fact versus opinion as a means of establishing appropriate use of relevant historical evidence. In this section, we will add another element to this process

by asking you to make supportable inferences about sources—a key skill in evaluating evidence about the past.

To review, an inference is an educated guess based on the information provided. To formulate an inference, you must go *beyond* the information given and suggest theories about an author's possible motives, point of view, and purpose that are not explicitly stated in the material. Moreover, you must establish connections between what is stated and what is left unstated in a source. When done correctly, these hypotheses are grounded in the document and will help to place the source in a larger context.

This is an important skill in the AP U.S. History redesign because it allows you to evaluate documents beyond the level of simple narrative. An inference demonstrates in-depth thinking about the purpose, point of view, and intended audience of a source. Rather than simply reporting the content of a source, you propose application, analysis, and evaluation of the document, demonstrating a deeper understanding of a historical issue or problem.

Practicing the Skill

Directions: Examine the following document and review the possible inferences that could be made about it. Notice that while the ideas are based on the source, they are not explicitly stated within it.

Document 1

Source: *Northwest Ordinance*, 1787

1. Congress shall appoint a governor, a secretary and three judges for the Northwest Territory. These officials shall adopt suitable laws from the original states. When the territory has 5,000 free male inhabitants of full age they shall be allowed to elect representatives.... .

2. The inhabitants shall be entitled to the benefits of trial by jury and other judicial proceedings according to the common law.

3. Religion, morality and knowledge being necessary to good government and happiness of mankind, schools ... shall forever be encouraged.

4. There shall be neither slavery, nor involuntary servitude in the said territories, otherwise than in the punishment of crimes whereof the party shall have been duly convicted.

Inferences:

a. The nation was expanding.

b. Americans wanted written rules of government.

c. Statements of rights had political importance.

d. Women did not count politically.

e. Education was important.

f. Concerns about slavery existed.

Applying the Skill

Directions: Below is a document about the Alien and Sedition Acts. After you read it, make a list of inferences that are suggested by the text. Write your inferences in your notebook.

Document 2

Source: Octavius Pickering and Charles Wentworth Upham, *The Life of Timothy Pickering*, 1873

The Alien Law has been bitterly criticized as a direct attack upon our liberties. In fact, it affects only foreigners who are plotting against us, and has nothing to do with American citizens. It gives authority to the President to order out of the country all aliens he judges dangerous to the peace and safety of the United States, or whom he suspects of treason or secret plots against the government.... .

The Sedition Act has likewise been wrongly criticized as an attack, upon freedom of speech and of the press. On the contrary, it allows punishment only for disturbers of order "who write, print, utter or publish any false, scandalous and malicious writings against the government of the United States, or either house of the Congress ... or the President..."

What honest person can justly be alarmed at such a law? Who can wish that unlimited permission be given to publish dangerous lies...? Because we have the right to speak and publish our opinions, it does not necessarily follow that we may use it to utter lies about our neighbor or government. After all, freedom of action does not give us the right to knock down the first person we meet and excuse ourselves from punishment by pleading that we are free persons...

Inferences:

Chapter

10

Contextualizing Events

A s you study AP United States History, it's
important that you do not view events
in isolation. Rather, they must be connected
to contemporaneous and/or background
developments. In other words, it is necessary
to establish their **context**. By placing an event in its larger place and time, you
make its importance clearer and more meaningful to a reader.

REASONING SKILL

• Contextualization

While the factors leading up to a specific topic may not always serve as its
primary cause, acknowledging events related to it will provide a perspective
that gives greater clarity to its importance. Contextualization is also an
antidote to simply listing facts one right after another without meaning
or significance. Dealing with the larger constellation of developments will
strengthen your written work and demonstrate that you see events in a more
complex fashion. Overall, establishing the context of events is all about
connecting and enriching your argument.

On the pages that follow you will see the factors that established the context
for writing the Articles of Confederation in 1776–1777. Study the example
and discuss it with your class or study group. After you have finished your
discussion complete the exercise by contextualizing the developments around
the concept of "salutary neglect."

Practicing the Skill

Directions: Look at the prompt below concerning the writing of the Articles of Confederation. Discuss with your classmates how the pre-1776 ideas influenced the writing of the Articles, and if additional ideas should be added to either side of the chart.

> **Example Prompt:** *Analyze the events, beliefs, and practices from 1763–1775 that set the stage for the writing of the Articles of Confederation in 1776–1777.*

Pre-1776 Ideas	Elements and Principles of the Articles of Confederation
• tension from the French and Indian War	• executive power was a danger to liberty
• king not an ally but enemy	• power should be at local level
• distant governments endangered rights	• taxation was a threat to liberty
• taxes (Stamp Act, Tea Act) unfair	• standing armies dangerous to rights
• control trade at individual colonial level	• power of purse must be at the local level
• clashes with troops (Boston Massacre)	• colonies regulate internal/ external trade
• governors detached from people	• states' sovereignty must be preserved
• English rights under attack	• minimal cooperation among colonies
• limited colonial cooperation to win goals	

Applying the Skill

Directions: Examine the prompt below and fill out the chart as a preparation to answering the question.

Exercise Prompt: *How was England's decision to end salutary neglect in the 1760s a reflection of the growing division between the colonies and the mother country?*

Relationship *during* Salutary Neglect Era	Relationship *after* Salutary Neglect Era

Chapter

11

Analyzing Secondary Sources

Historians often describe, analyze, and evaluate different versions of the past. They look at the same event through different intellectual lenses and interpret the evidence according to their individual perception of those events. As such, each historian has their own **point of view**.

DISCIPLINARY PRACTICE

- Analyzing Evidence (Secondary Sources)

If possible, try to identify the historian with a specific school of thought about the topic. That is, do they subscribe to a well-known interpretation (revisionism, traditional, post-revisionism, etc.) of an event? Your teacher may provide you with this type of background.

On the Short-Answer Question (SAQ) section of the exam, you may be asked to explain a historian's point of view and how it is supported. In this chapter, you will look at an interpretation of the French and Indian War to begin this explanation process. In the following Practicing the Skill section, you should read the selection carefully and study the interpretation of the author's point of view that follows. With the second excerpt, you will make your own determination of the author's point of view.

For more information about Short-Answer Questions, turn to page 197 of Appendix B.

Practicing the Skill

Directions: Look at the excerpt below (Document 1) about the result of the French and Indian War. After careful consideration of the document, study the example point of view analysis provided.

Document 1

> **Source: Fred Anderson and Andrew Cayton, *The Dominion of War*, 2005.**
>
> "If the Seven Years' War has lessons to teach us today, they may well center on the degree to which a decisive victory can be more perilous for the victor than the vanquished....The destruction of the French empire in North America laid the foundation for an unprecedented assertion of imperial authority when a series of British ministers pursued administrative and fiscal reforms that first baffled, then angered, the king's North American subjects. ... The irony is as obvious as it is instructive: the unintended consequence of the greatest military triumph of the eighteen century was the self-immolation of the triumphant empire in a revolutionary civil war."

Point of View:

The author believed that the war was deleterious to England in the long run, even though it "won" the war. Great Britain's position in the world was harmed rather than improved, and the conditions generated by the war helped to bring on the American Revolution.

Applying the Skill

Directions: Look at the passage below (Document 2) and determine the author's point of view about the result of the French and Indian War. Also, compare this passage with the excerpt above (Document 1), and then discuss how the historians behind the two excerpts disagree about the results of the war.

Document 2

Source: Francis Parkman, *The Seven Years War*, 1968.

"Thus in the war [French and Indian] just ended two great conditions of success had been supplied: a people instinct with the energies of ordered freedom, and a masterly leadership to inspire and direct them. All and more than all, that France had lost England had won. Now, for the first time, she [England] was beyond dispute the greatest maritime and colonial Powers. Portugal and Holland … had long ago fallen hopelessly behind…. It is true that a heavy blow was soon to fall upon her [England]…But nothing could rob her of the glory… ."

Point of View:

Unit 4

The Jeffersonian Era & the Age of Jackson

"The Celeste-al Cabinet"
— lithograph by A. A. Hoffay, 1836

Period 4: 1800–1848

Period Summary

Thomas Jefferson's election over John Adams was the first transition from one political party to another. Unlike the Federalists, the Democratic Republicans supported a limited, frugal government. Jefferson's primary goals were reductions in the central government, the national debt, the excise tax, and the military. The overall thrust of his governance was to increase the agrarian, states' rights influence of his constituents. The purchase of Louisiana in 1803 was the main plank in his achievement of these goals.

The latter half of the period was dominated by Andrew Jackson and his ideas. Jacksonians glorified individualism, declared war on privilege, vowed to restrain the federal government, and promoted states' rights—all this with an eye to the interests of southern and western farmers. He and his allies opposed the re-charter of the national bank, backed down a tax revolt in South Carolina, and opened the Deep South by moving Native Americans westward into Oklahoma. Jackson's use of presidential power—especially his numerous vetoes—prompted the rise of a second party system. The opposition to Jackson took the name Whigs, and would be an effective political force until the early 1850s.

Ideas for Discussion

1. How did the Louisiana Purchase change America's future?

2. Could one argue the War of 1812 was a senseless waste of resources and men? Why or why not?

3. How was the "Era of Good Feelings" a misnomer?

4. How did the election of Andrew Jackson represent the rise of the common man?

5. How did the struggle over the Second National Bank symbolize the ideals of Jacksonian democracy?

Extend Your Understanding

For a complete review of Period 4: 1800–1848 and more Ideas for Discussion, scan the code or go to
www.sherpalearning.com/skillbook/review/unit-4

Using Graphs and Maps Effectively

Earlier we investigated the importance of using relevant evidence by separating fact from opinion and drawing inferences from documents. In this section, we will expand these skills by describing and evaluating how to use visual materials as evidence.

DISCIPLINARY PRACTICE

• Analyzing Evidence

Graphs and maps are a staple of most AP history textbooks and often appear as sources for DBQ essays. They are especially popular in the multiple-choice section of the redesigned exam. Graphs and maps should be analyzed in a consistent and effective manner in a fashion similar to how traditional text-driven documents are analyzed.

For the most part, you probably look at these types of sources at an enumeration level. That is, you observe the data as an ordered listing of all the items in a collection of related content. For example, your examination might reveal things like territories acquired, battle sites, the dollar amount of exports, and various other demographics.

While this information is important, maps and graphs can be more useful when you think beyond the limits of the content presented. The ability to extract relevant information and draw appropriate conclusions from visual sources requires you to analyze the material on a higher level. You need to **extrapolate** and **hypothesize** about the visuals, and then **draw inferences** from them—much the same as you would do for text-driven documents, like essays and letters.

To use maps more analytically, ask and answer any of the following questions that apply:

1. Does the map suggest factors, trends, or developments that you had not previously considered about the topic? What are they?

2. What groups would benefit or be hurt by the changes shown by the map?

3. On a political map, for which political group is the map good news? For which is it bad news?

4. According to the map, what geographic region is changing? What cultural, social, or economic impact might result from these changes?

5. What is the central point or idea of the map?

6. What questions are left unanswered by the map?

Likewise for graphs, you might ask any or all of the following:

1. What trends does the graph trace?

2. Who would benefit from these trends? Who would be hurt?

3. For a political graph, what partisan problems or opportunities does it suggest?

4. What relationships or connections among events or factors can you infer from the graph?

5. What is the central point or idea expressed by the graph?

6. What questions are left unanswered by the graph?

Practicing the Skill

Directions: Examine the map and graph concerning the election of 1800 shown on the next two pages. Think about how these two sources and the questions about them expand your knowledge and understanding of this controversial election. In your notebook, write a paragraph about how the map and graph expanded your knowledge of the election of 1800.

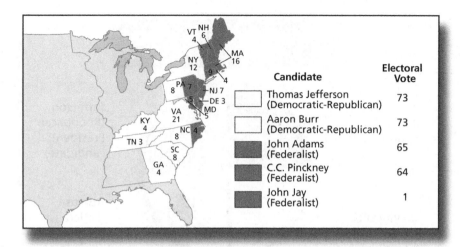

Candidate	Electoral Vote
Thomas Jefferson (Democratic-Republican)	73
Aaron Burr (Democratic-Republican)	73
John Adams (Federalist)	65
C.C. Pinckney (Federalist)	64
John Jay (Federalist)	1

1. **What economic groups do you think supported the Republicans? The Federalists?**

The Republicans could count on agrarian interests in the South and West. The Federalists had support from commercial and fishing interests in the Northeast.

2. **How does this map undermine the idea that Thomas Jefferson was president of ALL the people?**

Jefferson's support was geographically limited to the South and West. He needed to repair political relationships in the Northeast.

3. **For which political party is the map good news? For which group is it bad news? Why?**

The Republicans were likely to see their power grow as the nation expanded westward. The Federalists did not have good future prospects because they were unable to expand outside the Northeast.

4. **What other questions could you ask about the map?**

What policies did the Republicans support to appeal to the South and West? Was there any way for the Federalists to win back the White House in 1804?

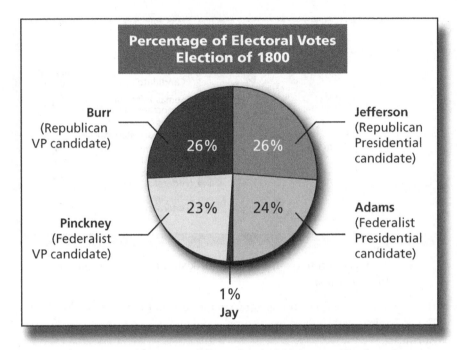

1. Since Aaron Burr was Jefferson's running mate, what does the graph tell us about the method of electing the president in 1800?

Since the two men tied for the presidency, which was not the intended outcome for Republicans, the system prescribed in the original Constitution for electing the president needed change, and it was modified under the 12th Amendment.

2. How did the results of the election make it difficult for Jefferson to claim a mandate for change in 1800?

Jefferson barely won the election. He only received 26 percent of the electoral vote and his Federalist opponent, John Adams, got 24 percent. In fact, without the three-fifths compromise, Jefferson would have lost to Adams.

3. What does the graph tell you about the political appeal of the two parties in 1800?

The nation was still closely divided in 1800. The Republicans won 52 percent of the electoral vote and the Federalists got 47 percent. The election was not a mandate for either party.

4.   Who were the "losers" in the election of 1800?

The Federalists were the losers; the New England commercial and mercantile interests also could not have been happy with a southern slave holder back in the White House.

5.   What other questions about the election does the graph suggest?

Why were the Federalists unable to expand their appeal to the South and the West? What Constitutional crisis did the results create? What role did Aaron Burr play in resolving the crisis?

Applying the Skill

Directions: Examine the map showing the Louisiana Purchase and the graph that shows the history of American exports from 1790 to 1815. Answer the questions about each visual source, and then write a short paragraph about how the two sources expanded your knowledge and understanding of events occurring from 1800 to 1815. Write your answers in your notebook.

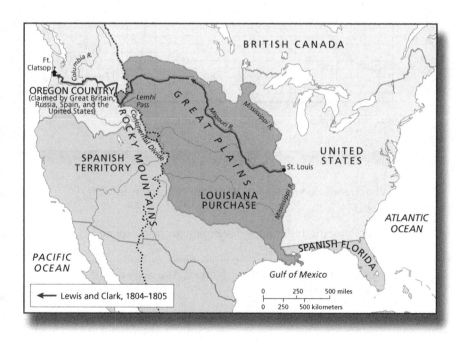

1. What economic and foreign policy advantages did the United States gain from the Louisiana Purchase?

2. Which parts of the United States benefited most from the purchase? Why?

3. What groups of people in the United States were hurt by the purchase? Why?

4. How did the purchase make America a stronger nation?

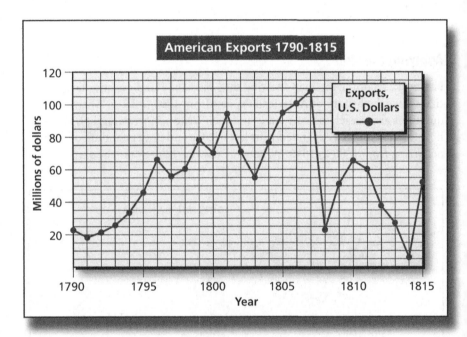

1. What trends do you see for American exports from 1790 to 1815?

2. What domestic and foreign developments help explain these trends?

3. What conclusions can you reach about American exports from 1790 to 1815?

Establishing Point of View

In another part of the book we introduced the skill of interpreting documents using **H.I.P.P.O.** In this section we will expand on one of those elements—the first **P.** in **H.I.P.P.O.**, point of view. Much of United States history is the story of clashing points of view between individuals and groups.

A point of view is a position or attitude that a person (or group) takes on an issue or event. It can be closely related to the second **P.** in **H.I.P.P.O.**—the purpose of the document. Often, point of view is a perspective that influences acceptance or rejection of ideas and actions. By determining an individual's point of view, you can come to understand their motivation and add depth to your analysis of their thinking and actions.

When you understand point of view, you can also identify patterns. Patterns can help you understand causes like, for example, why certain individuals joined together to form political, social, and economic alliances, and how factions and interest groups grew. In many cases, the structure of an entire historical period is revealed through point of view. As you analyze one person's views and compare it to others, you delve into the origins of both agreements and disagreements in a historical period.

Practicing the Skill

Directions: To practice the skill of analyzing points of view, you will focus on the clashes between Andrew Jackson and John C. Calhoun. In order to make this analysis, you will compare and contrast the two men's positions according to the following prompt:

> **Example Prompt:** *What events helped alienate John C. Calhoun from Andrew Jackson in the 1820s and 1830s?*

First, examine the chart shown on the opposite page. The issue of Tariff of Abominations has been addressed. Jackson was against tariffs in general, but would not lower them until the national debt was extinguished. Calhoun held a very strong opinion against tariffs for the reason that they did not advance southern economic development in any way.

Applying the Skill

Directions: Copy the chart on the following page into your notebook, and then complete the chart by filling in the spaces for the other five issues. Decide whether each man supported the event and/or the action it represented; or opposed the event and/or the action it represented. Also write a short statement explaining why the two men took the position they did on each item. Finally, draft a brief response to the original question.

Did Jackson and Calhoun support or oppose the following?

Issue	Jackson's Point of View	Calhoun's Point of View	Discussion
Tariff of Abominations	Mildly Opposed	Strongly Opposed	Jackson opposed high tariffs in general, yet felt they were necessary until the national debt was paid. Calhoun believed tariffs hurt the South, and feared the growing power of the central government.
The Market Revolution			
Nullification of laws			
Indian Removal Act			
Exposition and Protest			
Use of the Spoils System			

Chapter

14

Using Documents in an Essay

In Chapter 5 we introduced the first four parts of the **H.I.P.P.O.** strategy to interpret primary sources. In this section, we will deal with the fifth part of the anagram—the process of <u>O</u>rganizing and employing one of the four elements to support an argument in a DBQ essay. Once you have established

a document's historical context, intended audience, and point of view or purpose, it is critical to organize one facet of the source and use it—along with outside information (facts not mentioned in the documents)—to bolster your argument. In order to score high on this type of essay, both documents and outside facts must be employed.

Documents can be cited in one of two fashions. If you are using an idea from part of a source, it should be referenced with quotation marks around it. However, because the redesign rewards the use of six documents, you should also include a document label—such as (Doc. 1) if you are citing Document 1 —at the end of the quote. This will help the reader as they count the number of documents you have used. If, on the other hand, you plan to use the general idea expressed in the source, you may paraphrase the content, but again, put (Doc. 1) at the end of your sentence to show where the idea came from.

Practicing the Skill

Directions: Study the example prompt and document below about the causes of the War of 1812, along with the explanation of the document's point of view. The example demonstrates how the document is organized and employed to express the author's point of view.

Example Prompt: *"To what extent did America go to war in 1812 to resolve issues beyond maritime rights?"*

Document 1

Source: Felix Grundy, *Annals of Congress*, 12th Congress, 1811

For my part I am not prepared to say that this country shall submit to have her commerce interdicted or regulated by any foreign nation. Sir, I prefer war to submission.

Over and above these unjust pretensions of the British Government, for many years past they have been in the practice of impressing our seamen, from merchant vessels; this unjust and lawless invasion of personal liberty calls loudly for the interposition of this Government.

By quoting Felix Grundy, a student can effectively establish his or her point of view that not only were America's economic interests threatened by British action, but its honor and pride were injured as well.

One possible way for using the entire idea of the passage to demonstrate this position would be to write the following:

> "In 1812, War Hawks such as Felix Grundy had had enough of British interference with United States shipping. These actions not only caused economic hardships, but also wounded

America's pride. Grundy joined many in Congress in advocating war to solve the problem (Doc. 1)."

A second way to use the document to establish Grundy's point of view is to quote selectively from the passage. A student using this method might write the following:

"In 1812, Felix Grundy made clear that America would not allow its 'commerce interdicted or regulated by any foreign nation.' The action not only hurt America economically, but was also an 'unjust and lawless invasion of personal liberty' and made some Americans 'prefer war to submission' (Doc. 1)."

Always remember that documents are there to help prove your point. They are pieces of information to be used—along with outside information—to address the question being asked.

Applying the Skill

Directions: Begin by studying the exercise prompt and Document 2 below. Identify the point of view expressed by John Quincy Adams in the document and consider how you can utilize the document to support the statement in the prompt. Finally, create two draft responses according to the tasks shown below. Be sure to include document labels in both responses!

Exercise Prompt: *"To what extent was the Monroe Doctrine designed to protect not only the Western Hemisphere, but American nationalism, as well?"*

Document 2

Source: John Quincy Adams, *Memoirs*, Philadelphia, 1875

The object of Canning appears to have been to obtain some public pledge from the government of the United States, ostensibly against the forcible interference of the Holy Alliance between Spain and South America; but really or especially against the acquisition to the United States themselves of any part of the Spanish American possessions.... . By joining with her, therefore, in her proposed declaration, we give her a substantial and perhaps inconvenient pledge against ourselves and really obtain nothing in return.

1. In your notebook, draft a brief response to the prompt (two or three sentences) using the entire idea of the document to capture Adams's point of view.

2. Next, draft a brief response using several quotes from the document to capture Adams's point of view.

Chapter

15

Using Contrasting Documents

When the College Board redesigned the course and exam, they introduced the skill of synthesis. But on the May 2015 AP U.S. History examination, less than 16% of test-takers earned this point on their DBQ response. Lucky for you, **synthesis was removed from the exam** with the Summer 2017 revisions. Nevertheless, it remains a valuable skill and can serve as an effective way to strengthen your historical arguments.

> **DISCIPLINARY PRACTICE**
> - **Argument Development**

Synthesis is the ability to develop new understandings of the past by applying insights to broader historical contexts or events. A means to do this is to develop new perspectives on a topic or event by recognizing contrary evidence between primary sources, and then connecting it to another context, period, or discipline.

On the DBQ in particular, there may be sources that challenge each other, or that refute the thrust of a prompt completely. These contradictions should not be ignored; they are an important factor in the argumentation process. By acknowledging their presence in the evidence, you establish historical complexity. According to the revised DBQ rubric, you can earn one of two Analysis and Reasoning points by "qualifying or modifying an argument by considering diverse or alternative views or evidence."

However, be careful that you do not refute your thesis completely. A rebutting document can be effectively used alongside other documents in a sentence, or—if the document represents a major contrary position—it may require a paragraph near the end of the essay that more fully accounts for the challenge to the thesis. This concession paragraph might modify your thesis, but must not overturn it.

By including these documents, you demonstrate to the reader your ability to think like a historian by acknowledging the complexity of the issue that you are addressing.

Practicing the Skill

Directions: Examine the prompt below about the Market Revolution that unfolded during the Age of Jackson. Then, look at the two documents on the following page related to the Market Revolution's social and economic impact.

Below you will find a sample paragraph that could, in part, answer the statement. As you will see, while the two documents have contrary views on the impact of commercialization on America, they can be woven together to support a topic sentence. In a complete essay, the contrasting documents could occupy an entire paragraph.

Example Prompt: *To what extent did the Market Revolution strengthen the economic and social fabric of the United States as it developed in the first half of the 19th century?*

Document 1

Source: J. S. Buckingham, *America, Historical, Statistic, and Descriptive,* 1841

But among them all there were fewer than perhaps in any other community in the world who live without any ostensible avocation. The richest capitalists still take a part in the business proceedings of the day; and men who have professedly retired and have no counting-house or mercantile establishment still retain so much of the relish for profitable occupations that they mingle freely with the merchants, and are constantly found to be the buyers and sellers of stock, in funds, or shares in companies, canals, railroads, banks, et cetera. The result of all this is to produce the busiest community that any man could desire to live in.

Document 2

Source: Harriet Hanson Robinson, *Loom and Spindle: Life Among the Early Mill Girls,* 1898

Cutting the wages was not the only grievance, nor the only cause of this strike. Up till now the corporation had paid 25 cents a week toward the board of each worker. Now it intended to have the girls pay the sum. This, in addition to the cut in wages, would make a difference of at least one dollar each week. It was estimated that as many as 1,500 girls went on strike and walked as a group through the streets. They had neither flag nor music; instead, they sang songs, a favorite one being:

"Oh, isn't it a pity, such a pretty girl as I—should be sent to the factory to pine away and die?"

Example Paragraph: While the Market Revolution of the 1830s produced great wealth and progress in the nation, its impact was uneven and unfair. The commercial developments made New York capitalists rich and powerful as they mingled "freely with merchants, and [were] constantly found to be the buyers and sellers of stocks...." On the other hand, the women of Lowell faced great hardships when their wages were reduced to the point where they wondered if they "should be sent to the factory to pine away and die." This issue of wealth disparity would bedevil the nation throughout the rest of the 19th century and into the 20th century. It would be the impetus for economic and social reforms of the Progressive Movement and the New Deal as well.

As you can see, the two documents present different views of the impact of the Market Revolution in America. It was possible, however, to use both documents in the same paragraph by structuring the topic sentence to suggest that while progress occurred, it was not evenly spread across the society. The issue of wealth disparity is then connected to other historical contexts and eras.

Applying the Skill

Directions: Look at the statement below and the two documents that accompany it. In your notebook, write a paragraph that uses both documents to support your argument. Then, try to connect the issues raised to other historical contexts or periods.

Exercise Question: *"John C. Calhoun is often viewed as the voice of discord and sectionalism."*

To what extent is this assessment accurate for the career of John C. Calhoun from 1817 to 1833?

Document 3

Source: John C. Calhoun, *Works*, February 1817

Let it not be said that internal improvements may be wholly left to the enterprise of the states and individuals. I know that much may justly be expected to be done by them; but, in a country so new and so extensive as ours, there is room enough for all the general and state governments and individuals in which to exert their resources. But many of the improvements contemplated are on too great a scale for the resources of the states or individuals... .They require the resources and the general superintendence of this government to effect and complete them... .

Document 4

Source: *South Carolina Exposition and Protest*, December 19, 1828

"The Senate and House of Representatives of South Carolina ... solemnly Protest against the system of protecting duties...

5th.   Because, from the Federalists ... it is clear the power to regulate commerce was considered by the Convention as only incidentally connected with the encouragement of agriculture and manufactures...

6th.   Because, whilst the power to protect manufactures is nowhere expressly granted to Congress, nor can be considered as necessary and proper to carry into effect any specified power, it seems to be expressly reserved to the states, by the 10th section of the 1st article of the Constitution."

Developing a Thesis

DISCIPLINARY PRACTICE
- Argument
  Development

On several occasions we have examined elements of creating a strong written argument in an AP class. Here, we will enlarge this skill by focusing on developing a strong thesis. A thesis statement is a critical part of writing effectively on both the Document-Based Question (DBQ) and Long Essay Question (LEQ) in AP U.S. History. In fact, when you examine the rubrics, or grading standards, used to evaluate these essays (Chapter 37), you will see that the first thing a reader is instructed to look for in any answer is a strong thesis statement. The thesis should appear early in the first paragraph of the essay, ideally as the first sentence. And it must do more than restate the question; it must make a historically defensible claim. Some students underline the thesis statement to make certain their paper clearly focuses on their argument, and to ensure that anyone evaluating their paper can easily see what position they are taking in answering the question.

The first step to developing strong, effective thesis statements is to be sure you fully understand the objectives of a thesis. A thesis statement is all of the following:

1. a controlling idea around which your paper is built

2. a one-sentence answer to the historical question being asked

3. a concise statement of your essay's argument

4. a point of view adopted about a historical problem

5. a proposition to be defended or argued

The basic elements of a strong thesis include a statement that accomplishes the following:

1. It deals with all aspects of the topic suggested by the question.

2. It takes a clear position on the issue.

3. It provides an organizational framework from which to structure your essay.

4. It addresses the core issues defined by the question (i.e., is on target).

One way to evaluate your thesis statement is to check if it passes the **A.C.I.D.** test. An effective thesis should include/accomplish each of the following:

★ The A.C.I.D. Test

A. <u>A</u>ll aspects of the topic addressed

C. <u>C</u>lear position on the issues

I. <u>I</u>nfrastructure to build on

D. <u>D</u>irectly target the question

Practicing the Skill

Directions: Look at the following statement and the three thesis statements offered. Each thesis statement represents a possible beginning to a response to the prompt.

Example Prompt: *"The utopian societies of the 1830s and 1840s formed in response to the social and economic upheavals that affected America after the War of 1812."*

Assess the validity of this statement.

Possible Thesis Statements:

Thesis 1: There were many changes in America after the War of 1812 that gave rise to utopian societies.

Thesis 2: The emerging Market Revolution, increasing urbanization, and immigration after the War of 1812 promoted the rise of utopian societies.

Thesis 3: The rise of Jacksonian democracy, the common man, and the abolitionist movement made many people seek alternative lifestyles in the 1830s.

By applying the **A.C.I.D.** test to each of the statements, we can clearly identify which statement is the best.

- Statement 1 is too general. It does not identify the changes that affected America, give a structure for the essay, or address the core economic and social issues. It does take a weak position on the question, however.

- Statement 3 is a weak thesis statement because it is off topic. There is a danger that it will take the paper in the wrong direction. Following it, a writer is likely to drift into politics and abolition. It may address utopian societies—but only in a secondary way. On the positive side, it does take a position and provides an organizational framework. In fact, it is actually a good thesis... for a different question!

- The best thesis statement is statement 2. It passes the A.C.I.D. test. It deals with economic and social issues; it takes a clear position that these factors caused utopian societies to form; it provides an organizational framework to the structure of the essay (i.e., Market Revolution, growth of cities, impact of immigration); and it deals with the topics suggested by the question.

Applying the Skill

Directions: Study the prompt and evaluate the three thesis statements that follow. Apply the **A.C.I.D.** test to make a determination as to which statement is the strongest start for discussing the statement in the prompt.

Exercise Prompt 1: *"Although the end of slavery was an agreed upon goal, the abolitionists were divided over the best means to achieve it."*

Assess the validity of this statement.

Possible Thesis Statements:

Thesis 1: William Garrison wanted to use moral persuasion to end slavery and other abolitionists wanted to form political parties to achieve an end to slavery.

Thesis 2: The abolitionists wanted to end slavery, but did not know exactly how to do it.

Thesis 3: While the abolitionists wanted to end slavery, they disagreed over the political, social, and economic means to do it.

Which thesis statement did you select? Why did you select this thesis statement? Write your answers in your notebook. After making your choice, discuss it with your classmates or your study group members.

Next, write a thesis statement for the following prompt in your notebook and then compare your statement with those of your classmates or members of your study group.

Exercise Prompt 2: *"The abolitionist movement was both a catalyst and a hindrance for the women's rights movement."*

Assess the validity of this statement.

Contextualization and Chart Analysis

A nother challenging skill to master on the redesigned AP U.S. History examination is contextualization. Contextualization calls upon students to connect events or sources to broader regional, national, or global processes within the time period under consideration. It involves creating larger constellations of development that bear some influence on the

DISCIPLINARY PRACTICE

• **Analyzing Evidence**

REASONING SKILL

• **Contextualization**

topic under consideration. You must associate events or sources to what else was happening during the time and that might be, in some way, related to the event(s) being evaluated.

One possible—though often overlooked—source that can be used to help contextualize an answer is charts. Not all of the seven sources in a DBQ are texts; along with photographs and cartoons, charts are often included in a DBQ as potential evidence for your argument. Beyond argumentation, though, charts can be effectively used to provide contextualization. To do this, a chart must first be **a)** analyzed systematically, and then **b)** related to broader phenomena within the time frame of the question.

During the exam in May, you won't be able to spend a great deal of time on any one source during the DBQ preparation period (the recommended duration is 15 minutes—see Appendix B on page 194 for more information). Having a consistent plan for analyzing data-rich charts will give you a decided advantage. When you see a chart, think of the **5 Ts**!

★ **The 5 Ts**

T1. **Time period being examined**—Remember, contextualization requires that all connections be made to larger processes within the chronological parameters of the question.

T2. **Topics presented**—What item(s) do you see in the chart?

T3. **Trends in the chart**—Are there consistent tendencies? Inconsistent tendencies?

T4. **Tie trends to causes**—Hypothesize about the causes of the trends.

T5. **The implications (of trends)**—What larger process or circumstance is suggested by the chart? (Contextualization)

Practicing the Skill

Directions: Look at the chart below about the ratio of slaves to cotton production during the 19th century. Then, follow along as the **5 Ts** are applied to this chart.

Year	Bales of Cotton	Number of Slaves
1810	178,000	1,103,700
1820	335,000	1,509,904
1830	732,000	1,983,860
1840	1,348,000	2,481,390
1850	2,136,000	3,200,364
1860	3,846,000	3,950,511

Source: *Historical Statistics of the United States, Colonial Times to 1970*

Sample Application of the 5 Ts:

Time: 1810–1860

Topics presented: Cotton production and slavery

Trends in the chart: As cotton production increased, so did the need and demand for slaves

Tie trends to causes: The South became a one-crop cash area and more and more dependent on slave labor.

The implication of trends: Cotton was king by 1860. The cotton gin had revolutionized the crop's production and the need for slaves exploded, especially in the Deep South. Cotton and slavery dominated social, political, and economic life in the region and made it much more difficult to see slavery ended voluntarily, thus making armed conflict more likely in 1861. (contextualization)

Applying the Skill

Directions: Examine the chart below, and then complete the **5 Ts** in your notebook. Compare your answers with your classmates or with members of your study group.

Year	White Female Population (in thousands)	Children Under Age of 5 Born to Women Age 20–44 (per 1,000 white women)	Women 65 and Older (in thousands)
1810	2,874	1,358	n/a
1820	3,866	1,295	n/a
1830	5,171	1,145	209
1840	6,940	1,085	281
1850	9,526	892	408
1860	13,111	905	585

Source: *Historical Statistics of the United States, Colonial Times to 1970*

Time:

Topics presented:

Trends in the chart:

Tie trends to causes:

The implication of trends:

Unit 5

Manifest Destiny to Reconstruction

Engraving of Union troops recapturing artillery at the
Battle of Shiloh, Tennessee, April 6, 1862
—artist unknown

Period 5: 1844–1877

Period Summary

Responding to the transformation of American society after the War of 1812, there were crusades for improvements for the mentally ill and the establishment of alternative utopian societies. In addition, the abuses of alcohol generated one of the strongest reform movements of the 1830s and 40s. And, although in the shadow of the abolitionist crusade, the women's movement flickered to life at this time.

In the early 1840s, America increasingly viewed territorial expansion as a means to restore its confidence and prosperity lost during the Panic of 1837. The focus of expansion became Texas and its surrounding territories. Unable to resolve the Texas question, the U.S. and Mexico went to war in 1846.

Violence and political upheaval marred the second half of the 1850s. A mini-Civil War broke out in Kansas, and in 1857 the Supreme Court weighed in on the slavery debate with the Dred Scott decision. In 1859 John Brown roiled the nation with violence as he tried to incite a slave rebellion at Harpers Ferry, Virginia. Brown's raid convinced the South it could only remain safely in the Union by controlling the White House. That control vanished in 1860 when Abraham Lincoln was elected. After the election, eleven southern states left the union and the nation was thrown into Civil War.

Ideas for Discussion

1. What was the attitude toward the abolitionist movement in both the North and South in the 1830s and 1840s?

2. Was the Wilmot Proviso the first political shot of the Civil War? Explain.

3. Was Abraham Lincoln too slow to act against slavery during the Civil War?

4. Did Andrew Johnson deserve to be impeached? Explain why or why not.

Extend Your Understanding

For a complete review of Period 5: 1844–1877 and more Ideas for Discussion, scan the code or go to
www.sherpalearning.com/skillbook/review/unit-5

Extending and Modifying a Thesis

In the previous unit, we defined a thesis statement, identified its main elements, and suggested its best placement in an essay answer. In this section, we will address alternative ways a thesis can be expressed to answer an essay prompt. A thesis statement

is a one-sentence answer to a historical problem suggested by an essay question/statement. You may agree, disagree, or do a little of both when evaluating the validity of the prompt. Since the redesign of the course, you may now earn credit for contradiction, corroboration, and/or qualification in accounting for historical complexity. As a result, experience with a variety of thesis approaches will be very useful as you develop your argument. As long as you can defend your position, it is permissible to challenge the ideas expressed by the question/statement. It is, however, imperative that you be able to support your contrary positions with facts.

On one hand, you may agree with the ideas expressed in the prompt and write a positive thesis statement that supports the question/statement. For example, a prompt that suggests expansion into Texas and Oregon greatly influenced the outcome of the presidential election of 1844 is an accurate summary of the issues of the campaign. It would be answered with a positive thesis statement that affirms the validity of the prompt. This will advance your argument and can provide a strong beginning to your paper.

On the other hand, you may confront a question/statement that is an overstatement or even an inaccuracy about a historical event or phenomenon. In this case, you may disagree with the ideas expressed and write a negative thesis statement that challenges the ideas of the prompt. For example, a question/statement that suggests the Mexican War promoted American unity in the 1840s cannot be defended, and your thesis would negate the assertions being made.

A final possibility is a question/statement that is partially correct. It may express some ideas that you can defend and others with which you disagree. Here, you would use a positive/negative thesis—one that acknowledges both agreement and disagreement with the ideas expressed by the prompt. For example, an essay statement that credits the Compromise of 1850 with contributing to sectional harmony could only be accepted as partially accurate. While recognizing that the Compromise soothed tensions briefly, you would also need to point out that sectional conflict flared up again within four years. Thus, you would write a thesis that addresses both the positive and negative responses to the prompt.

Practicing the Skill

Directions: To practice writing positive, negative, and positive/negative thesis statements, look at the following essay prompts and their respective thesis statements. Notice that each prompt was first converted into a clarifying question and that the answer to that question became the thesis statement. By transforming the prompt into a question, you will be better able to decide the degree to which you agree or disagree with the ideas being expressed.

Example Prompt 1: *Evaluate the extent to which the Polk administration's policies toward Texas were the primary cause of the Mexican War.*

Clarifying Question: Did President Polk's policies cause the Mexican War?

Positive Thesis: President Polk's aggressive and warlike stance toward Texas annexation caused armed conflict with Mexico in 1846.

The writer agreed with the ideas in the prompt and will demonstrate that Polk's policies were responsible for causing the war.

Example Prompt 2: *Evaluate the extent to which popular sovereignty was an effective means to deal with the question of slavery in the territories.*

Clarifying Question: How effective was popular sovereignty in dealing with slavery in the territories?

Negative Thesis: Rather than promoting sectional harmony, the implementation of popular sovereignty became a divisive means of dealing with the question of slavery in the territories.

The writer does not agree with the prompt's statement about the effectiveness of popular sovereignty. He/she will use evidence to show how ineffective popular sovereignty was in resolving the slavery question in the territories.

Example Prompt 3: *Evaluate the extent to which Henry Clay's political decline impacted the nation and his place in history in the early 1850s.*

Clarifying Question: Did Henry Clay lose his political effectiveness and historical significance in the 1850s?

Positive/Negative Thesis: Although Henry Clay lost much of his political influence in the 1850s; he did author one last union-saving measure that solidified his place in history as "the Great Compromiser."

The writer recognizes that Clay was slipping in the 1850s, but notes that his role in compromise legislation from the 1820s through the 1850s cements his place in history.

Applying the Skill

Directions: Look at the following three prompts. For each prompt, write a clarifying question in your notebook, and then construct a thesis statement by answering the clarifying question. Write a positive thesis for the first prompt, a negative thesis for the second, and a positive/negative thesis for the third.

Exercise Prompt 1: *Evaluate the extent to which southern actions and demands from 1845-1855 reinforced the idea that a "slave power" existed in the United States.*

Clarifying Question:

Positive Thesis:

Exercise Prompt 2: *Evaluate the extent to which President Polk's "failure of nerve" cost America its achievement of the 54 degrees 40 minutes boundary of Oregon.*

Clarifying Question:

Negative Thesis:

Exercise Prompt 3: *Evaluate the extent to which the land acquired in 1848 damaged the United States more than it benefited the nation's development.*

Clarifying Question:

Positive/Negative Thesis:

Cartoons and Contextualization

In Chapters 10 and 17, we discussed how charts could serve as valuable pieces of evidence in a historical argument. We also suggested that when properly analyzed, they could be utilized to contextualize an essay response. Cartoons can serve a similar function, but like documents and charts, you must develop a consistent approach for utilizing them. These types of visuals play an increasingly important role on the AP examination. They frequently appear on the DBQ and now are regularly used as source material for the redesigned multiple-choice questions.

DISCIPLINARY PRACTICE

- **Argument Development**

REASONING SKILL

- **Contextualization**

Cartoons can be very difficult to analyze. When you look at this type of image, you are bombarded with data. Without topic sentences and paragraphs as organizational guides, you may go into "information overload" when trying to absorb everything presented in the cartoon all at once. You must dissect the cartoon piece by piece and see how the representation can be used as part of a DBQ response or to answer multiple-choice items.

You should approach a cartoon as you would any other type of historical source—establish a logical, step-by-step process for extracting and analyzing data. The strategy that follows provides a systematic approach to analyzing cartoons. By using it, you can identify the key elements of the visual and, ultimately, develop a summary of the cartoon's information—a skill that will prove extremely valuable in your AP class and later on the AP examination.

In addition, a cartoon—when appropriately addressed—can help contextualize your response to essay prompts. As was discussed earlier, contextualization asks you to relate information to large constellations of development, and to identify how an event is related to broader processes and phenomena. A cartoon can be employed to expand meaning beyond a specific event and yet place it in a clear historical context.

A useful strategy for regularly analyzing and contextualizing a cartoon is to "confront a cartoon **D.A.I.L.Y.**"

★ D.A.I.L.Y. Cartoon Analysis

When analyzing a cartoon, look for the following:

D. **D**ate of the cartoon—Hopefully you can go beyond the date and explain what else was happening at the time the events depicted in the drawing occurred. (contextualization)

A. **A**ction in the cartoon—What is going on inside the cartoon?

I. **I**mportant things in cartoon—What people/objects/places do you recognize? What was the significance of those things to the time period? (contextualization)

L. **L**abel of the cartoon—A label can be a title or caption. Does it support or contradict the action taking place? By comparing the Label to the Action, you can establish the author's point of view.

Y. **Y** (Why) the cartoon was created—What larger issues does it represent? (again, contextualization)

Practicing the Skill

Directions: Look at the cartoon on the next page and study how **D.A.I.L.Y.** could be applied. Discuss the cartoon with your classmates.

The People's Line--Take care of the Locomotive
Sold at 104 Nassau, and 18 Division Streets, New-York.

Date: The election of 1840.

Action: Van Buren campaign is stuck and breaking down because of Henry Clay's opposition and William Henry Harrison's efficient campaign.

Important People/Objects: Martin Van Buren, William Henry Harrison, the "influence" of Henry Clay, the hard cider campaign, the log cabin campaign.

Label: The People's Line--Take care of the Locomotive—the idea that the Harrison campaign is on track and forceful and Van Buren's campaign is faulting. (point of view)

Y (Why) Created: To support Harrison's campaign and its contrast to the sad state of Van Buren's effort in 1840 because of the Panic of 1837 and the Whig opposition led by Henry Clay. (contextualization)

Applying the Skill

Directions: Study the cartoon on the opposite page and use **D.A.I.L.Y.** to begin your analysis. Discuss your answers with your classmates or study group.

D̲ate:

A̲ction:

I̲mportant People/Objects:

L̲abel:

Y̲ (Why) Created:

"Political Climbing Boys," Anonymous, 1844

Chapter
20

Comparing and Contrasting Historical Positions

Earlier in this book, you worked on analyzing points of view for individuals through the use of charts. As you may recall, the exercise for that lesson (Chapter 13) asked you to evaluate the different positions of John

C. Calhoun and Andrew Jackson, and to explain their alienation in the 1830s. Through the chart, you focused on how contrary views defined individuals and their points of view. In this section, we will expand on this by comparing not only differences, but similarities between people and events, and observe how these comparisons can expand your understanding of the past.

By investigating both converging and diverging beliefs and characteristics, you will add depth and complexity to your historical study. By establishing similarities and differences, you can develop generalizations about how individuals and groups had different experiences with the same event or issue. You will come to understand how similar and contrasting positions on topics evolved and affected both ideas and actions.

One effective means of analyzing similarities and differences is through a Venn diagram. This device consists of two circles that delineate similarities (overlapping sections) and differences (the sections that do not overlap). The advantage of this simple tool is that it clearly lays out both variances and commonalities. In addition to providing useful information for answering comparison questions, they can also effectively supply supportive and rebuttal evidence for arguments. Further, the tool allows you to group information into new patterns of meaning that may not have been apparent before you placed the facts and ideas into the diagram.

★ Venn Diagram

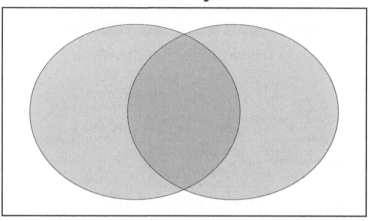

Practicing the Skill

Directions: Examine the example prompt below. Then, review the diagram with your classmates and discuss how it might serve as an outline for answering the prompt.

> **Example Prompt:** *"If the North and South had exchanged presidents, the South would have achieved its independence."*
>
> *Assess the validity of this statement.*

The statement suggests that Abraham Lincoln possessed greater leadership abilities than Jefferson Davis during the Civil War. One way to assess the validity of the prompt is to create a Venn diagram that evaluates how the two men differed in terms of their attributes and beliefs. You can strengthen your analysis of the two leaders, however, by also assessing the similarities they shared. This will add depth to your answer and make your response stronger and more complete.

On the next page you will find a sample Venn diagram that makes such an analysis.

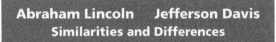

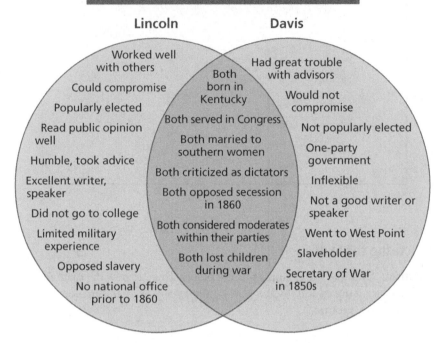

Abraham Lincoln   Jefferson Davis
Similarities and Differences

Lincoln   Davis

Worked well with others

Could compromise

Popularly elected

Read public opinion well

Humble, took advice

Excellent writer, speaker

Did not go to college

Limited military experience

Opposed slavery

No national office prior to 1860

Both born in Kentucky

Both served in Congress

Both married to southern women

Both criticized as dictators

Both opposed secession in 1860

Both considered moderates within their parties

Both lost children during war

Had great trouble with advisors

Would not compromise

Not popularly elected

One-party government

Inflexible

Not a good writer or speaker

Went to West Point

Slaveholder

Secretary of War in 1850s

Applying the Skill

Directions: Below is another prompt about the Civil War and Reconstruction era. Examine the prompt, and then, in your notebook, create a Venn diagram in which you outline the similarities and differences between Andrew Johnson and his critics between 1865 and 1869.

Exercise Prompt: *"Despite some early cooperation, Andrew Johnson and the Radical Republicans ultimately clashed over the direction of Reconstruction between 1865 and 1869."*

Assess the validity of this statement.

Using Documents and Charts in an Essay

As you proceed through the rest of this book, you will notice that the exercises begin to build on earlier activities, expanding upon the Disciplinary Practices and Reasoning Skills you are developing, and eventually combining various skills and practices together with the ultimate goal of writing effective DBQ and LEQ essays. In this section, for example, you will explore how to combine two sources—a chart and a document—in your essay. Keep in mind that in order to score high on the DBQ, you must make use of six sources in your response. The ability to combine two sources is a stepping-stone in that process.

DISCIPLINARY PRACTICE

- **Analyzing Evidence**

REASONING SKILLS

- **Change over Time**
- **Contextualization**

We have introduced strategies for dealing with documents (**H.I.P.P.O.**) and charts (**5 Ts**), and now we will put the two pieces of evidence together and organize/apply them to support a thesis. Also, in constructing your response you must address at least one of the following from the material: historical context, intended audience, point of view, and/or purpose. It is important to demonstrate how one of these four aspects—found in each piece of evidence—is employed in your answer.

Practicing the Skill

Directions: On the pages that follow are two sources on southern Reconstruction governments—a chart of state constitutional conventions (1867–1868) and a report by James Pike on South Carolina's legislature in 1868. Analyze both the chart and the report with the **5 Ts**.

Document 1

Membership of State Conventions, 1867–68							
State	**Black**	**%**	**White Native**	**%**	**Northern**	**%**	**Total Members**
Alabama	18	17%	59	55%	31	28%	108
Arkansas	8	13%	35	52%	23	35%	66
Florida	18	40%	12	27%	15	33%	45
Georgia	33	19%	128	74%	9	7%	170
Louisiana	49	50%	*	*	*	*	98
Mississippi	17	17%	29	29%	54	54%	100
N. Carolina	15	11%	100	75%	18	14%	133
S. Carolina	76	61%	27	22%	21	17%	124
Virginia	25	24%	33	31%	47	45%	105
Texas	9	10%	*	*	*	*	90
							* *information not available*

In analyzing the chart you should see the following:

- Except in South Carolina, African Americans did not represent a majority in the conventions.

- "Negro domination" of the process was a myth.

- "Carpetbaggers" were a minority in every convention, except Mississippi.

- Whites (southern and northern) were in the majority in every convention, except South Carolina.

- The chart contradicts the idea of a southern political revolution.

- The chart adds context to the idea of Reconstruction as revolutionary.

Document 2

Source: James Shepherd Pike, *The Prostrate State: South Carolina Under Negro Government*, 1874

The blacks outnumber the whole body of whites in the House more than three to one. On the mere basis of numbers in the State the injustice of this … is manifest since the black population is relatively four to three of the whites. A just correction of the disproportion, on the basis of population, merely, would give fifty-four whites to seventy black members… .

One of the first things that strike a casual observer in this negro assembly is the fluency of debate … The leading topics of discussion are well understood by the members… . When an appropriation bill is up to raise money to catch and punish the Ku-klux [sic], they know exactly what it means… . The [Negro legislator] will speak half a dozen times on one question, and every time say the same things without knowing it. He answers completely to the description of a stupid speaker in Parliament… .

But underneath all this shocking burlesque upon legislative proceedings, we must not forget that there is something very real to this uncouth and untutored multitude… . Seven years ago these men were raising corn and cotton under the whip of the overseer. Today they are raising points of order and questions of privilege. They find they can raise one as well as the other. They prefer the latter… . It means liberty… .

In reading Pike, you should understand that he:

- looked at one state—South Carolina

- found black domination in legislature—although the chart counters that this was rule throughout the South

- believed Blacks understood the debate and looked after their interest

- saw Blacks had trouble with legislative procedures

- found that underneath the "shocking burlesque" of legislative procedures, liberty was stirring

- was expressing his point of view about Reconstruction politics

Using the two sources and outside information, a paragraph was constructed as a partial answer to the following prompt:

Example Prompt: *Evaluate the extent to which the participation of African Americans revolutionized southern politics from 1865 to 1877.*

Possible Thesis: While Reconstruction brought many changes to the South, Black voting failed to revolutionize southern politics from 1865–1877.

Sample Paragraph: As a result of the 13th, 14th, and 15th Amendments, a significant number of black men participated in the new southern governments. Furthermore, as noted in the chart, they were active in creating the new state constitutions mandated under Radical Reconstruction, but they did not dominate the process. (Doc. 1) (historical context) Moreover, while observers such as James Pike found a "shocking burlesques upon legislative proceedings" in South Carolina, he also saw that Blacks were able to understand the debate and were working toward greater liberty. (Doc. 2) (point of view)

The paragraph, using data from the chart, Pike's report, and outside information, demonstrated the limited, but complex role that African Americans played in certain phases of Reconstruction politics. To add to the idea of continuity and change during the years 1865–1877, you might cite the on-going resistance to changes in the South as Blacks voted and discuss the election of 1876, which marked an end to Radical Reconstruction. The use of the two sources together helped temper the impression of "Negro rule" in the early part of Reconstruction and added a complexity to the treatment of this important era of American history.

Applying the Skill

Directions: Study the prompt below and the two sources on the next page. Extract information from each source and, in your notebook, write one paragraph that could be a partial answer to the prompt. With both sources, make sure you focus on **at least one** of the following: historical context, intended audience, point of view, and/or purpose.

After you have compared your answer with classmates or members of your study group, consider other ideas that might be included in your paragraph.

Exercise Prompt: *Discuss the impact of slavery on the economic and social life of the South from 1850 to 1860.*

Document 3

Source: Hinton Rowan Helper, *The Impending Crisis of the South: How to Meet It*, New York, 1857

It is a fact well known to every intelligent Southerner that we are compelled to go to the North for almost every article of utility and adornment, from matches, shoe pegs, and painting up to cotton mills, steamships and statuary, that we have not foreign trade, no princely merchants, nor respectable artists. ... Whilst the free states retain not only the larger proportion of those born within their own limits, but induce, annually, hundreds of thousands of foreigners to settle and remain amongst them ... owning to the absence of a proper system of business amongst us, the North becomes in one way or another, the proprietor and dispenser of all our floating wealth... .

Document 4

Source: *Historical Statistics of the United States, Colonial Times to 1970*

Region	Persons in Manufacturing		Urban Population as % of Total Population of Region	
	1850	1860	1850	1860
Northeast States	574,307	734,134	27.2%	36.0%
North Central States	86,834	143,055	9.7%	13.8%
Southern States	59,154	68,960	7.0%	8.7%

Unit 6

America
Transformed

Doffers in Cherryville Mfg. Co.,
North Carolina, November 1908
—photograph by Lewis Wickes Hine

Period 6: 1865–1898

Period Summary

From the end of the Civil War to the turn of the century, Americans headed west. For millions of settlers farming remained the American Dream, however, farmers faced a world far different from the agrarian conditions that existed before the war. The years after the Civil War witnessed explosive industrial growth as well. In 1869, there were 2 million factory workers; by 1899 that number more than doubled to 4.7 million.

Industrialization produced a growing urban working class. Factory and service workers grew to 51 percent of the labor force by the turn of the century. A "new immigration" flooded into the cities, and by 1900, some 40 percent of the U.S. population lived in urban areas. Workers increasingly turned to labor unions to improve their conditions.

A growing resentment amongst farmers against the political establishment gave rise to the Granger Movement (1870s), the Farmers' Alliance (1880s), and the Populist Party (1890s). The 1890s were a tumultuous decade, with the Populists providing the political sparks and the nation suffering through its deepest depression of the century. But expansionist ideas began to build in the 1890s, and a "New Manifest Destiny" swept the nation.

Ideas for Discussion

1. How did the Populist Party reflect deep dissatisfaction among many Americans with their government?

2. How were trusts a blessing and a curse for America?

3. How did the expansionist impulse of the 1890s compare with such ideas and events in the 1840s?

4. Was the Big Stick policy short-sighted in promoting America's long-range interests in South America? Explain your answer.

5. How did the Philippine insurrection expose the flaws in the "New Manifest Destiny" of the 1890s?

Extend Your Understanding

For a complete review of Period 6: 1865–1898 and more Ideas for Discussion, scan the code or go to www.sherpalearning.com/skillbook/review/unit-6

Recognizing Relevant Evidence

Throughout this book you have examined the use of relevant evidence in developing your writing skills by separating fact from opinion, drawing inferences from documents, and unlocking meaning from graphs and

DISCIPLINARY PRACTICE
• Analyzing Evidence

maps. In this chapter, you will work on evaluating evidence that is most relevant to support your response to a prompt. If you use information that is not relevant in answering the question, you create several problems. There is a danger that you might completely miss the point of a question when you use evidence that is off target. For example, your sources may not address the topic at hand, or fail to address the specific focus of the question, which leads to a jumbled and confused response. All this can result in composing a great answer to the wrong question, resulting in a low score. In the exercises below, you will examine relevant versus irrelevant evidence by establishing standards to apply in determining the relative value of information.

When weighing the relevance of information, you should keep the following criteria in mind:

1. Does the evidence deal with the correct time period?

2. Does the evidence target the issues being investigated?

3. Does the evidence focus on the specific aspect of the topic that is being evaluated?

For example, when looking at the question "How did the battle over currency standards define politics after the Civil War?" a student should use information from the years 1865–1898 that deals with economics and politics and concentrates on the struggle between supporters of silver and gold.

Practicing the Skill

Directions: Below is a question about the loss of black rights from 1877–1898. The question is followed by four statements that might be used to support it. After looking at the question and the statements with your classmates, discuss the relevancy of each piece of evidence in answering the prompt. Then look at the discussion provided about the relevant value of each statement in support of a sound answer.

Example Prompt: *Explain the causes and consequences of the "betrayal of blacks" from 1877 to 1898.*

Statement 1: The rise of Jim Crow led to political and economic suffering for African Americans from 1877 to 1900.

Statement 2: The abolitionists tried for many years to end slavery, and they finally succeeded in helping improve the lives of African Americans.

Statement 3: President Woodrow Wilson had a record of racial injustice while he was president that damaged the lives of many African Americans.

Statement 4: The Supreme Court ruling in *Plessy v. Ferguson* ended the promise of Reconstruction for African Americans.

Sample Evaluation:

Statement 1 is relevant. It is about the years of Reconstruction, and it deals with the loss of civil rights for African Americans.

Statement 2 is irrelevant. It is about the abolitionist movement that preceded Reconstruction and does not deal with the later loss of rights.

Statement 3 is irrelevant to the question. It is about the years between 1913 and 1921. While it is an accurate statement about Wilson's policies, it does not have a direct bearing on the betrayal of African Americans after the Civil War.

Statement 4 is relevant. The case was decided in 1896 and directly influenced the loss of political, social, and economic rights for African Americans.

Applying the Skill

Directions: Below is another question about the period from 1865 to 1898. The question is again followed by four statements that might be used to support it. Read the question and the statements carefully and determine the relevancy of each piece of evidence in answering the prompt. Then, look at the discussion provided about the relative value of each statement in supporting a sound answer to the question. Write your responses in your notebook.

Exercise Prompt: *How did the Populist Party reflect deep dissatisfaction among many Americans with their government?*

Statement 1: The Populist demands for regulation of the food industry finally forced the government to act.

Statement 2: The Populists supported government regulation of railroads throughout the 1880s and 1890s.

Statement 3: When the Populists got the government to pay farmers for surplus crops, agrarian life became easier and better.

Statement 4: The Populist demand for expansion of the money supply called attention to the problem of deflation after the Civil War.

Using Facts to Support a Thesis

A critical element in writing a strong, persuasive essay is the use of facts to support your thesis. We have already discussed the elements and variations of a thesis (Chapters 16, 18) and the differences between facts and opinions in building your argument (Chapter 1). In this section we will expand on those ideas and demonstrate the importance of using facts in your answer.

DISCIPLINARY PRACTICES

- **Analyzing Evidence**
- **Argument Development**

When responding to an essay prompt, you must offer more than opinions and generalizations. As mentioned earlier, an opinion is a belief or impression that is not based on concrete evidence. Opinions are often expressed as vague generalities that treat issues in a global fashion. If you write in this manner, you will appear lacking the necessary information to deal with the prompt, and be unable to convince an AP reader of the validity of your answer.

In order to score high on both the DBQ and the LEQ you must provide specific, appropriate, factual information in defending your thesis. Often on the AP examination, students cite only opinions and generalizations in supporting their point of view and fail to employ concrete examples that prove their assertions. By using facts rather than opinions, you establish credibility as someone who understands the historical problem posed by the prompt. You cannot do this with unsubstantiated ideas and vague generalities.

Practicing the Skill

Directions: Look at the essay prompt, the sample thesis statement, and the three statements used to support the thesis. Before reading the evaluation of the three statements, consider whether each is specific, appropriate, and factual.

Example Prompt: *Evaluate the extent to which the ideals of the Declaration of Independence were an unrealized dream for African Americans from 1877 to 1898.*

Sample Thesis: From 1870 to 1900, African Americans were promised equal justice, due process, and voting rights, but neither the North nor the South kept this pledge.

Statement 1: The Compromise of 1877 and the removal of northern troops played a major role in the betrayal of African American rights after the Civil War.

Statement 2: The South took rights away from African Americans that were promised by Radical Republicans.

Statement 3: Blacks should have fought harder for their rights after the Civil War.

The first statement is factual and provides solid information about the factors that led to the Jim Crow system of inequality. The second statement is a generalization about the period after the war and offers an impression without specific references to the actual events. The third statement is a personal opinion about the behavior of African Americans in the years 1865–1898.

Applying the Skill

Directions: Look at the two prompts below, their theses, and the three statements to support them. For each prompt, select the strongest statement in support of the thesis and explain, in your notebook, why it is the most effective. Discuss your choices with your classmates or with the members of your study group.

> **Exercise Prompt 1:** *Evaluate the extent to which the industrialists of the last quarter of the 19th century were visionaries, rather than "robber barons."*

Sample Thesis: The industrialists advanced America economically, but their greed gave them a deserved reputation for lawlessness and ruthlessness. (negative thesis statement)

Statement 1: Industrialists such as John D. Rockefeller and Andrew Carnegie did many good things and some bad things, but generally, they helped America become great.

Statement 2: Men such as John D. Rockefeller and Andrew Carnegie should have shared their money with more people, including their workers.

Statement 3: The trusts created by Rockefeller and Carnegie made America competitive internationally, but they exploited their workers and the American public.

Exercise Prompt 2: *Evaluate the extent to which the Populists' program of the 1890s offered acceptable solutions to the problems in American society.*

Sample Thesis: Farmers in the 1890s realized that America needed to reform, but their call for massive government actions and free silver kept them out of power.

Statement 1: Farmers were really hurting in the 1890s, and the Populists wanted to help them, but they went about it in the wrong way.

Statement 2: The Populist ideas of income taxes, immigration restrictions, and government ownership of utilities were popular with some people, but were too radical for most voters.

Statement 3: The Populist Party was ignorant to join up with the Democrats in 1896 because Bryan did not know what he was doing.

Using Documents and Cartoons in an Essay

In Chapter 19, you were introduced to cartoon analysis (**D.A.I.L.Y.**) with the goal of extracting information from a drawing and contextualizing its meaning. In this section, you will engage in a more complex activity—unlocking data from a cartoon and incorporating it into an essay along with a document. Remember that cartoons serve as historical evidence and are commonly found

on DBQs and as sources in the redesigned multiple-choice section. For this reason, you must be able to determine their meanings and understand them on multiple levels.

Further, in Chapters 5 and 14, we discussed the strategy of **H.I.P.P.O.** as a tool to interpret, organize, and apply documents in a response to a historical problem. Now, we will combine the processes of cartoon and document analysis, and utilize them together as a partial answer to a prompt (much like we did in Chapter 21 for documents and charts).

The cartoon and document below are about politics around the turn of the 19th century. Both offer perspectives about the relative importance of corruption in government as a political issue. In addition to the sources, there is a prompt that asks you to evaluate the role honesty in government played in the political process of the era and why the issue was important to the electorate. A thesis concerning the prompt is proposed, along with a sample paragraph as a partial answer for the problem. Notice that in the paragraph, information is drawn from both sources to support the writer's thesis.

Practicing the Skill

Directions: Study the prompt and the thesis, and then read through the sample paragraph. Next, examine the two documents that follow on pages 104 and 105, and consider the lists of information provided about the cartoon and the document. Finally, reread the sample paragraph, this time paying careful consideration to how the documents were used in combination to address the prompt.

Example Prompt: *Evaluate the extent to which politicians lived under the shadow of Ulysses Grant's presidency from 1876 to 1898.*

Sample Thesis: The scandals of the Grant administration and the issue of honesty in government became a dominant political issue for an entire generation.

Sample Paragraph: The scandals of the Grant administration and the issue of honesty in government became a dominant political issue for an entire generation. After the misdeeds and malfeasance of the 1870s, the voters demanded honesty from their political leaders. When James Blaine ran in 1884 for president, he was portrayed as a faker who tried to fool the people into believing he was a crusader or "Plumed Knight." In fact, he had been accused of using his office for private gain. (Doc. 1) (point of view, contextualization) Moreover, some political bosses tried to justify their actions by saying there was a difference between honest graft, which involved using insider information and did not hurt anyone specifically, and dishonest graft, practiced by those officials who took payoffs from saloon keepers and gamblers. (Doc. 2) (purpose, point of view) The voters rejected this distinction and demanded politicians protect the public interest rather than enrich themselves. (intended audience, point of view)

Document 1

Source: Thomas Nast, from "Harper's Weekly," August 9, 1884

THE "GREAT AMERICAN" GAME OF PUBLIC OFFICE FOR PRIVATE GAIN.
This is not "*Protection*"; this is *very* "*Free Trade*" with the people's money.

After using **D.A.I.L.Y.**, you should see in the cartoon that:

- Blaine tried to present himself as the "Plumed Knight," a crusader and reformer;

- the cartoon is satirizing this view of Blaine; (point of view)

- Blaine's background was tainted with scandal; (contextualization)

- he had a fake horse, lance, and breastplate;

- he used political office to gain public money;

- some saw politics as a game of seeking riches and promoting private interest.

Document 2

Source: George Plunkitt, "How I Got Rich by Honest Graft," 1905

Everybody is talking these days about Tammany men growing rich on graft, but nobody thinks of drawing the distinction between honest graft and dishonest graft. There's all the difference in the world between the two. Yes, many of our men have grown rich in politics. I have myself. I've made a big fortune out of the game and I'm getting richer every day, but I've not gone in for dishonest graft—blackmailing gamblers, saloon-keepers, disorderly people, etc.—and neither has any of the men who have made big fortunes in politics.

… My party's in power in the city, and it's going to undertake a lot of public improvements. Well, I, tipped off, … I see my opportunity and I take it. I go to the place and I buy up all the land I can in the neighborhood. … Ain't it perfectly honest to charge a good price and make a profit on my investment and foresight? Of course it is. Well that's honest graft.

After using **H.I.P.P.O.**, you should see that Plunkett believed:

- it was okay to use public office for private gain; (point of view)

- honest graft did not have specific victims; (his point of view)

- dishonest graft did hurt specific people;

- some officials practiced dishonest graft by taking payoffs from saloon keepers and gamblers, etc.; (historical context)

- using political office to gain advantage and insider information was fine; (point of view)

- he tried to justify different types of graft; (purpose)

- it is the American political way to see opportunities and take them;

- his point of view was widespread among politicians, but under attack during this time. (contextualization)

Applying the Skill

Directions: For the exercises below, you will find a prompt, a document, and a cartoon. Complete an information list for each source using the appropriate strategy (**H.I.P.P.O.** or **D.A.I.L.Y.**) as the basis for your analysis. Next, draft a thesis that accurately responds to the prompt. Finally, write a paragraph in your notebook that partially addresses the prompt using data from the cartoon and the document, as well as some outside information.

Exercise Prompt 1: *In 1896, William McKinley was presented as the solid statesman and William Jennings Bryan as the radical upstart. To what extent was this a fair description of the two men?*

Document 3

Source: William Jennings Bryan, speech at Democratic National Convention, 1896

You come to us and tell us that the great cities are in favor of the gold standard; we reply that the great cities rest upon our broad and fertile prairies. Burn down your cities and leave our farms, and your cities will spring up again as if by magic; but destroy our farms and the grass will grow in the streets of every city in the country...

... If they dare to come out in the open field and defend the gold standard as a good thing, we will fight them to the uttermost. Having behind us the producing masses of this nation and the world supported by the commercial interests, the laboring interests and the toilers everywhere, we will answer their demand for a gold standard by saying to them: You shall not press down upon the brow of labor this crown of thorns, you shall not crucify mankind upon a cross of gold.

Document 4

Source: W. A. Rogers, from "Harper's Weekly," August 29, 1896

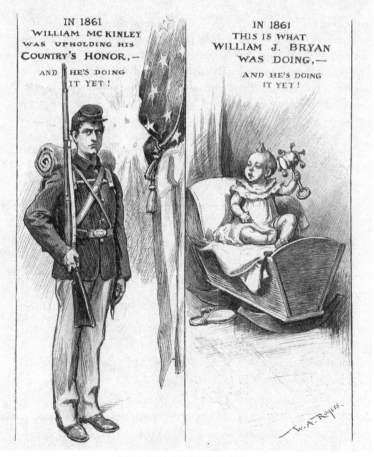

Exercise Prompt 2: *To what extent did the actions and policies of the federal government change the lives of African Americans from 1865 to 1898?*

Document 5

Source: John Marshall Harlan's dissent in *Plessy v. Ferguson*, 1896

In respect of civil rights, common to all citizens, the Constitution of the United States does not, I think permit any public authority to know the race of those entitled to be protected in the enjoyment of such rights…. I deny that any legislative body or judicial tribunal may have regard to the race of citizens when the civil rights of those citizens are involved…. We boast of the freedom enjoyed by our people… But it is difficult to reconcile the boast with a state of the law which, practically, puts the brand of servitude and degradation upon a large class of our fellow citizens, our equals before the law. The thin disguise of "equal" accommodations for passengers in railroad coaches will not mislead anyone, or atone for the wrong this day done…

Document 6

Source: Alfred R. Waud, "The First Vote," from "Harper's Weekly," November 16, 1867

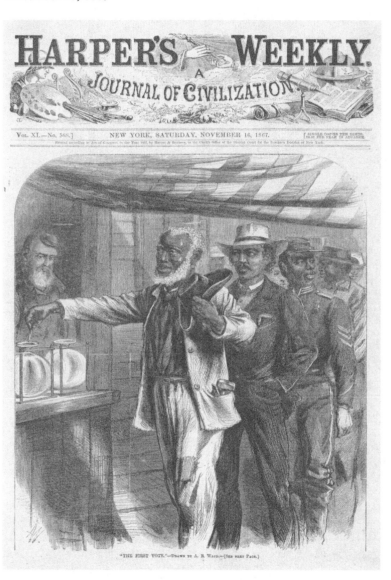

Unit 7

America
& the World

*Wreckage of the USS Arizona at Pearl Harbor,
December 7, 1941*

Period 7: 1890–1945

Period Summary

By 1900, America was a troubled nation. The urbanization and industrialization of the late 19th century damaged the country's social, economic, and political systems. To combat these problems, progressive reformers stepped forward to change America. Presidents Theodore Roosevelt and Woodrow Wilson implemented the 4 Cs of change. Overall, the reforms were rather modest, yet they were a first step to ending the laissez-faire philosophy of government and promoting social justice.

In 1914, Germany and the Central Powers challenged France and England for dominance in Europe. The U.S. declared its neutrality at the outset of the conflict. By 1917, however, America was pulled into the war by the Germans' use of submarines. President Wilson hoped America could "make the world safe for democracy."

When World War I ended, Americans were jolted by changes and challenges. The 1920s became a battleground between those who accepted change and those who longed for the past. Few groups experienced more changes in the 1920s than women, who received the right to vote with the 19th Amendment.

The decade of the 1920s ended with a stock market collapse and the onset of the Great Depression. While FDR's main concern in the 1930s was economic recovery, he watched with alarm as the Axis Powers seized territory and prepared for war. His indecision ended when the Japanese attacked Pearl Harbor, prompting the U.S. entry into World War II.

Ideas for Discussion

1. How did the progressive reformers try to make government more responsive to the people's interest?

2. How did the American value system change in the 1920s?

3. How was President Hoover's approach to ending the Depression both conservative and liberal?

4. How was the New Deal both a success and a failure?

Extend Your Understanding

For a complete review of Period 7: 1890–1945 and more Ideas for Discussion, scan the code or go to
www.sherpalearning.com/skillbook/review/unit-7

Bias and
Point of View

Elsewhere in the book, you analyzed how establishing point of view could be useful in answering a question that asks you to compare and contrast people's opinions and actions (Chapter 13). Now we will expand on that skill by discussing the role bias plays in determining an individual's point of view and

purpose in responding to a problem or issue. One of the first places to look in trying to explain a person's position and motivation on a topic is to examine their possible leanings toward it. An individual's viewpoint on an event or phenomenon, or their purpose for responding to or addressing it, is often affected by the inclinations they possess about it. In this chapter, you will go "behind the scenes" and examine how backgrounds, societal roles, and predispositions affect individual stances on issues. In short, you will look at the ways bias operates on historical figures as they formulate their beliefs and positions on various issues.

Dealing with bias is part of studying history. Bias is the presentation and support of facts in predetermined patterns of understanding. Most likely, the author of your textbook and even your teacher possess some degree of historical bias. Everyone brings a pre-conceived viewpoint of events that will—to some degree—color their interpretation of what happened in the past. People filter history through the prisms of religion, race, gender, education, and ethnicity. Their attitude and purpose can also be affected by office-holding, partisanship, and personal interest in the outcome of events.

While you cannot eliminate bias in studying history, you can recognize it and develop strategies for managing it. One way to deal with bias is to perform a "bias audit" in examining a person's stance on events and issues. When trying to determine bias, ask yourself the following four questions:

1. Did the individual hold an office that influenced their position? (This is an old saying – "Where one stands on an issue depends on where one sits.")

2. Did they have a personal stake in the decision or outcome of the event?

3. What purpose did they have in promoting their views?

4. Did their race, religion, education, or ethnicity affect their point of view or purpose?

Practicing the Skill

Directions: Look at the following question. Then, think about how the following individual would answer this statement and to what degree bias might be reflected in his/her response.

> **Example Prompt:** *Evaluate the extent to which the Philippine insurrection exposed the flaws in the "New Manifest Destiny" doctrine of the 1890s.*

William McKinley

Answer: President McKinley would say the New Manifest Destiny doctrine was not flawed.

Bias: He was basically the author of the policy, and he approved the crushing of the Filipino insurrection. His ownership of the policy and political position would support the ideas of expansion. He would not condemn his own policy. His purpose in support of the doctrine was to justify his own decision and action in keeping the Philippines.

Applying the Skill

Directions: Using the same prompt as above, determine how each of the following individuals would answer the statement and what bias/purpose might be reflected in their response. Write your answers in your notebook.

Exercise Prompt: *Evaluate the extent to which the Philippine insurrection exposed the flaws in the "New Manifest Destiny" doctrine of the 1890s.*

---

1. **Emilio Aguinaldo**

    Answer:

    Bias:

2. **Josiah Strong**

    Answer:

    Bias:

3. **George Dewey**

    Answer:

    Bias:

Interpreting Secondary Sources

The skill of Analyzing Evidence—as defined in the redesigned AP U.S. History curriculum—is complex, with a number of facets involved in its mastery. In Chapter 11, you began this process by looking at how historians' interpretation of events can differ.

You examined two divergent points of view about the results of the French and Indian War, and the relationship of those results to interpretation of the historical record. In this section, we will apply that skill more precisely to the format of the exam.

In your AP U.S. History class, as well as on the AP exam in May, you will encounter the notorious new question format introduced in the 2015 course redesign (and revised in the 2017 update)—the Short-Answer Question (SAQ). These items require you to write short, focused responses to a problem. They will comprise three tasks that are to be addressed using specific facts and details. The first SAQ will ask you to analyze excerpts from secondary sources usually involving debates between historians with differing points of views about a single topic or event. The materials will be drawn from periods 3–8 in the course curriculum. It will be your job to identify differing points of view and provide factual support for each position taken in the two sources.

With a question about a historical debate, there will be three sections that require you to identify the main points of each historian's interpretation, to recognize differences between the writers, and to cite specific examples that support or refute the positions taken. The prompt will always be divided into parts a, b, and c. It is advisable to label each part of your answer accordingly to make it easier for your teacher—or an AP reader—to evaluate your work.

Practicing the Skill

Directions: Look at the two statements below about American expansion in the 1890s. After reading the selections, examine the sample answers for parts a, b, and c and discuss them with your classmates or your study group members.

McKinley assumed power with the promise of restoring prosperity and the hope of ending the Cuban struggle.... . Fortunately, however, the administration would not fight these battles alone. An American business community that learned to think in world-wide terms during the 1890s would also devote its attention to restoring good times, stifling the Cuban disturbance, and maintaining the open door.... . McKinley and the business community worked in tandem.... . A friendly government would provide leadership. And inside that government the center of power would be found at the White House.

— **Walter LaFeber,** *The New American Empire: An Interpretation of Expansion 1860–1898*, 1963.

...the observation must be made that the rise of an expansionist philosophy in the United States owed little to economic influences. Of the writers mentioned, only [Alfred] Mahan had much to say of expansion as an aid to commerce, and Mahan's ideas were derived from the study of history, not from any contemporary economic pressure. In fact, as will be shown later, business interests in the United States were generally opposed to expansion, or indifferent to it, until May 1, 1898. The need of American business for colonial markets and fields of investment was discovered not by business men but by historians and other intellectuals, by journalists and politicians.

— **Julius Pratt,** *The Expansionists of 1898: The Acquisition of Hawaii and the Spanish Islands*, 1964.

Using the excerpts above and your knowledge of American history, answer parts a, b, and c.

   a)   Briefly explain ONE difference between LaFeber's and Pratt's interpretation of the causes of American expansion in the 1890s.

   b)   Briefly explain how ONE specific historical event or development in the 1890s could be used to support LaFeber's interpretation.

   c)   Briefly explain how ONE specific historical event or development in the 1890s could be used to support Pratt's interpretation.

Suggested Responses:

   a)   The two historians Julius Pratt and Walter LeFeber had differing views on the role of business and the White House in promoting expansion in the 1890s. Pratt believed business did not push or support expansion. On the other hand, LeFeber saw the business community as pushing expansion and that they received encouragement from the McKinley administration.

   b)   The depression of 1890s made business groups seek markets overseas to solve the economic problems at home. The Secretary of State, John Hay, had strong ties to business groups as did Elihu Root, Secretary of War. Root was, in fact, a former corporate attorney. Business groups had staged revolution in Hawaii in 1893. Coxey's Army frightened businessmen and they hoped expansion might solve the economic grievances of Coxey and his men.

   c)   Businesses in the 1890s were not monolithic. Some would benefit from expansion but others would be hurt if markets overseas were closed by armed conflict. Also, a leading industrialist, Andrew Carnegie, was active in the anti-Imperialist League. Many businesses saw that the economy was already recovering from the 1893 depression and did not want to rock the economic boat.

Applying Skill

Directions: Look at the two statements about the Progressive Movement on the next page, and then complete parts a, b, and c of the question that follows.

In diverse ways and with divergent goals, the progressive sought to modernize American institutions while attempting to recapture the ideals and sense of community that they believed had existed in the past. They battled conservatives, radicals, other reformers, and often each other. But despite their disagreements and difficulties, progressives played a major role in helping America adjust to new conditions and create new institutions for coping with the challenges of the time. They took the lead in establishing a social agenda for modern America.

— **John Chambers II,** *Tyranny of Change: America in the Progressive Era, 1890–1920,* **1992.**

...that the period from 1900 until the United States intervention in the war, labeled the 'progressive' era by virtually all historians, was really an era of conservatism... In brief, conservative solutions to the emerging problems of an industrial society were almost uniformly applied. The result was a conservative triumph in the sense that there was an effort to preserve the basic social and economic relations essential to a capitalist society, an effort that was frequently consciously as well as functionally conservative... .

— **Gabriel Kolko,** *The Triumph of Conservatism: A Reinterpretation of American History 1900–1916,* **1963.**

Using the excerpts above and your knowledge of American history, answer parts a, b, and c.

a) Briefly explain ONE difference between Kolko's and Chambers' interpretation of the Progressive Movement.

b) Briefly explain how ONE specific historical event or development in the years 1900–1917 could be used to support Kolko's interpretation.

c) Briefly explain how ONE specific historical event or development in the years 1900–1917 could be used to support Chambers' interpretation.

Grouping Documents into Categories

While extracting information from documents, charts, and cartoons is very important, you must also be able to sort the information you uncover into useful patterns. In other words, you must be able to place sources into categories.

A basic yet important grouping system for evidence is to create categories of *support for* and *opposition to* the thesis you intend to defend. On most DBQs, you will encounter some documents that affirm your position and others that challenge or even contradict the thrust of the prompt. Both types of sources must be identified and included when writing an essay answer.

After you have formulated your thesis, listed your outside information, determined the meaning of the sources, and established the context (or audience, or point of view, or purpose) of each item, you must then place the data into categories of support (pro) or opposition (con).

The quickest and most effective technique is to read the thesis carefully, examine each document, and then place a plus sign (+) beside all sources that you plan to use in support of your position and a minus (–) sign alongside all those that challenge the thesis. Once each document has been labeled, you should make a chart (see example on the next page) and list the documents that support the thesis on the plus side, and the contrary documents on the minus side. Don't try to write parts of the document into the chart; instead, list them by their document numbering. The chart will serve as a graphic organizer for the DBQ and can be expanded as you add outside information that supports or challenges the thesis.

Practicing the Skill

Directions: Below is a prompt about foreign policy in the 1890s, a suggested thesis statement, and four documents used as evidence in the answer. Each document has either a plus sign or a minus sign alongside it to indicate whether it supports or challenges some part of the thesis. Examine the sample documents, their placement in the chart, and the rationale for categorizing each one as either a pro or con source. Discuss the four documents and their categorization rationale with your classmates or in your study group.

Example Prompt: *Evaluate the extent to which in the 1890s many Americans realized the United States could not cling to its foreign policy of the past.*

Sample Thesis: Some Americans in the 1890s realized the nation must look to the future rather than the past, and accept a new international role.

(This thesis is supported by sources that present the political and economic benefits that expansion offered America. Sources that deal with the isolationist past would challenge the thesis.)

(+)   Document 1

Source: *The San Francisco Evening Bulletin*, January 30, 1893

Hawaii is the central point of the North Pacific. It is in, or near to, the direct track of commerce from all Atlantic ports, whether American or European. ... It is the key to the whole system. ... In the possession of the United States it will give us the command of the Pacific.

(–)   **Document 2**

> **Source: Letters of Grover Cleveland**
>
> I regarded, and still regard [he said] the proposed annexation of these [the Hawaiian] islands as not only opposed to our national policy, but as a perversion of our national mission. The mission of our nation is to build up and make a greater country out of what we have, instead of annexing islands.

(–)   **Document 3**

> **Source: *Public Opinion* (newspaper), Chambersburg, Pennsylvania, February 9, 1889**
>
> …The diplomatic service has outgrown its usefulness … It is a costly humbug and sham. It is a nurse of snobs. It spoils a few Americans every year, and does no good to anybody. Instead of making ambassadors, Congress should wipe out the whole service.

(+)   **Document 4**

> **Source: Congressional Record, 55th Congress, 2nd Session, Appendix**
>
> Manifest Destiny says, 'Take them [Hawaiian Islands] in.' The American people say, 'Take them in.' Obedient to the voice of the people, I shall cast my vote to take them in, and tomorrow this House of Representatives will by a good, round majority say, 'Take them in.'

Pro	Con
Document 1	Document 2
Document 4	Document 3

Sample Rationale: Document 1 supports expansion for economic reasons. It describes the commercial benefits the Hawaiian Islands would bring. Document 4 illustrates how popular expansion was with the people, and suggests how it was a winning political issue. Document 2 opposes expansion, stating that it goes against America's mission of building internally and avoiding world affairs. Document 3 also opposes involvement in the world by expressing the idea that the Foreign Service should be disbanded as it had no benefit to the people, and that the money could be spent more wisely elsewhere.

Applying the Skill

Directions: Study the prompt below about the struggle over the Treaty of Versailles, as well as the sample thesis statement and the four documents that follow. Each of the documents either offers support for the thesis or challenges some part of it. Label each document with a plus sign for *pro* or a minus sign for *con*. Create a chart in your notebook like the one shown on the previous page, and then place the document numbers into the chart. Finally, write a rationale for each document to justify its categorization.

Exercise Prompt: *Evaluate the extent to which Woodrow Wilson was responsible for the rejection of America for membership in the League of Nations in 1919–1920.*

Thesis Statement: While Woodrow Wilson's refusal to compromise over the Treaty of Versailles played a major role in keeping the United States out of the League of Nations, other people and events contributed as well.

( ) **Document 1**

Source: *Boston Herald,* **July 8, 1919**

AMERICANS, AWAKE

Shall We Bind Ourselves to the War Breeding Covenant?

It Impairs American Sovereignty

Surrenders the Monroe Doctrine!

Flouts Washington's Warning!

Entangles us in European and Asiatic Intrigues!

Sends Our Boys to Fight Throughout the World by Order of a League!

"The evil thing with a holy name."

( ) **Document 2**

Source: Woodrow Wilson's letter to the Senate, November 19, 1919

…In my opinion … the Lodge resolution does not provide for ratification but rather, for the nullification of the treaty. I sincerely hope that the friends and supporters of the treaty will vote against the Lodge resolution of ratification. I understand that the door will probably then be open for a genuine resolution of ratification.

( )   **Document 3**

Source: Henry Cabot Lodge speaks in Boston, March 19, 1919

[Article 10] pledges us to guarantee the political independence and the
territorial integrity against external aggression of every nation that is a
league member. That is, every nation of the earth. We ask no guaranties,
we have no endangered frontiers; but we are asked to guarantee the
territorial integrity of every nation, practically, in the world—it will be
when the League is complete. As it is today we guarantee the territorial
integrity and political independence of every part of the far-flung British
Empire. ... We, under the clause of this treaty—it is one of the few that
is perfectly clear—under that clause of the treaty we have got to take
our army and our navy and go to war with any country which attempts
aggression upon the territorial integrity of another member of the league.

( )   **Document 4**

Source: Wilson's letter to the Senate, March 8, 1920

Either we should enter the league fearlessly, accepting the responsibility
and not fearing the role of leadership which we now enjoy, contributing
our efforts towards establishing a just and permanent peace, or we should
retire as gracefully as possible from the great concert of powers by which
the world was saved.

Pro	Con

Creating an
Introductory Paragraph

A clear, well-formed introductory paragraph is vital to a successful essay answer. It not only introduces the reader to your argument and your thesis, but also serves as a road map for you to follow as you present your point of view in the body of the essay. Further, it prepares the reader for the ideas you plan to use in defense of your position. And while an introductory paragraph will narrow the focus of your paper, it can also serve to contextualize your argument by offering background that connects the main point of your essay to broader regional, national, or global processes.

DISCIPLINARY PRACTICE

- **Argument Development**

REASONING SKILL

- **Contextualization**

An introductory paragraph should contain the following elements:

- **Thesis Statement** – Your thesis, the position that you intend to defend, should appear early in the paragraph, preferably the first sentence when possible.

- **General Categories of Information** – Include the categories you plan to cite in proving your thesis. This will be one or two sentences that outline the problem posed by the prompt and how it will be addressed in the body of the essay.

- **Definition of Terms** – This may be necessary for some prompts, but not all. For example, if Theodore Roosevelt's liberalism is an issue in a question, you should use the introductory paragraph to establish a definition of liberalism.

- **Contextualizing Links** – As already mentioned above, a solid introduction should link the specifics of your paper to larger constellations of development that are connected to, and may influence the main topic of your essay.

- **Transitional Sentence** – A good introduction closes with a transitional sentence that links the introductory paragraph to the body of the paper.

The following elements do **not** belong in an introductory paragraph:

- **Specific Facts or Evidence** – Do not attempt to include specific details that support the thesis; this information is critical to your essay, but it belongs in the body of the paper. Remember that the opening paragraph should be a general overview of the answer.

- **Statement of Intentions** – Your intentions for the essay should not be expressed. For example, you should never write, "The purpose of this essay is…" or "In this essay I will…" Let the facts speak for themselves. If you have a strong thesis and substantial information to support your position, the reader will be clear on your position and intentions.

- **Apology** – Don't apologize. There is never any benefit to admitting a lack of knowledge or understanding about the prompt. Such an admission can only serve to prejudice the reader against your position at the outset of the essay.

- **Conclusion** – This might seem obvious, but be careful not to include a conclusion in the introductory paragraph. Don't try to do too much with the first paragraph. You will have an opportunity at the end of the paper to remind the reader of your thesis and how it was supported.

Practicing the Skill

Directions: Study the prompt on the next page and the paragraph that follows it. Try to identify the elements of a good introductory paragraph before reading the explanation that follows the sample introduction. Discuss the paragraph with your classmates or in your study group, and make sure that you can identify the key elements of an introductory paragraph.

Example Prompt: *Evaluate the extent to which President Theodore Roosevelt transformed American society from 1901–1909.*

Sample Paragraph: The years 1901–1909 were the apex of a reform movement known as the Progressive Era. Responding to the problems of growing industrialization and urbanization, individuals such as President Theodore Roosevelt took action to change America. While not a radical, Roosevelt made important reforms in America from 1901–1909. He expanded presidential powers, regulated trusts, preserved the environment, and protected consumers. All this made the country a better place to live. A review of Roosevelt's domestic policies will show his strong credential as a progressive reformer.

In this introductory paragraph, the writer gives background to the years in question, which contextualizes the answer. The paragraph also lays out a clear thesis that Roosevelt was a reformer but not a radical. It also presents the areas that will be discussed in the body of the paper: strengthening the presidency, trust busting, conservation, and consumer protection. Finally, it establishes that the paper will focus on Roosevelt's standing as a reformer.

Apply the Skill

Directions: Study the prompt below and write an introductory paragraph to address it. Make sure to include the essential elements of a beginning paragraph, as discussed above. After you have completed your paragraph, compare it with those of your classmates or your study group members.

Exercise Prompt: *Evaluate the extent to which the ideas and actions of Booker T. Washington contributed to maintaining continuity as well as fostered change in the lives of African Americans from 1895–1915.*

Writing a
Concluding Paragraph

A concluding paragraph is a vital but often overlooked element of a strong essay. In my many years scoring essays for the AP U.S. History exam, I have seen that—more often than not—students fail to leave enough time to write a conclusion, which can be extremely helpful in achieving a high score on an LEQ or a DBQ.

> **DISCIPLINARY PRACTICE**
> • Argument Development
>
> **REASONING SKILL**
> • Contextualization

A concluding paragraph should be brief and to the point, but provide closure to the paper. It is also another opportunity to add context to your argument. Here you can apply insights to your thesis by referencing another time or place. This can be very useful if you failed to add context earlier in your paper or wish to reinforce what you have provided to the reader.

A concluding paragraph should contain the following:

- A summary of the thesis statement; this should be a paraphrase of the original thesis and not an exact restatement
- One or two sentences that summarize the salient points used to prove the thesis

In certain cases, it may also contain the following:

- A review of the historical significance of the problem posed by the prompt; this is where a reference to other times and places can earn you the contextualization point
- A solution to the problem posed

A concluding paragraph should **not** contain the following:

- **New evidence or arguments** that were not in the body of the essay
- A **new thesis or point of view** that contradicts the original thesis
- An **apology** for not doing a better job in writing the essay

Practicing the Skill

Directions: Study the prompt below and the sample thesis that follows. Next, examine the sample paragraph provided. This paragraph would conclude the essay and a discussion of its elements. Compare the concluding paragraph to the bulleted lists in the preceding section to see each element in use. Then read the discussion explaining the sample. Finally, discuss the materials with your classmates or your study group members, with a focus on how the sample paragraph is an effective conclusion to the prompt.

Example Prompt: *Evaluate the extent to which the New Deal was both an economic success and a failure in the 1930s.*

Sample Thesis: Although the New Deal did not return the nation to pre-1929 prosperity levels, it successfully reduced suffering, promoted security, and restored faith in the American economic system.

Sample Concluding Paragraph: In summary, the New Deal did not bring about full economic recovery from the Depression in the 1930s; yet it reduced deprivation, and provided security for millions of Americans. Moreover, through the three Rs of Relief, Reform, and Recovery, it gave Americans hope and restored their faith in the capitalist system. In addition to its achievements, the New Deal reignited an on-going political and economic debate over the role of the government in society that would continue with the Great Society program of the 1960s and beyond into the new millennium.

The paragraph restates the thesis about how the New Deal succeeded and served the American people. The paragraph reminded the reader that the programs of the three Rs: Relief, Reform, and Recovery were the means by which the New Deal helped the country and restored confidence. We can presume that the body of the paper discussed specific programs such as the WPA, CCC, FDIC, Society Security, Wager Act, etc. Notice also that the conclusion tied the New Deal to the reforms of a later era—the 1960s and beyond (synthesis).

Applying the Skill

Directions: For the exercises that follow, use the prompt and the thesis statement to write a concluding paragraph that would serve as an effective summary for the thesis, and for the main ideas that would support it. Write your paragraphs in your notebook. Compare your concluding paragraphs with those of your classmates or with the members of your study group.

Exercise Prompt 1: *Evaluate the struggle between the isolationists and internationalists for control of United States foreign policy from 1935–1941.*

Sample Thesis: The isolationists dominated the American foreign policy debate from 1935–1939, but as military events in 1940–1941 frightened the nation, the internationalists became increasingly influential.

Concluding Paragraph:

Exercise Prompt 2: *Evaluate the extent to which the use of the atomic bombs in August 1945 was a political rather than a military act.*

Sample Thesis: While some people argued that the use of atomic weapons at the end of World War II was designed to influence Soviet behavior in Eastern Europe, the bombings were a military necessity that helped avoid an invasion of Japan, saving countless lives on both sides.

Concluding Paragraph:

Unit 8

The Cold War &
the American Dream

Levittown, New York,
—photo by Ezra Stoller, February 1955

Period 8: 1945–1980

Period Summary

At the end of war, neither the United States nor the Soviet Union relinquished its prewar views of world affairs. The Soviets clanked down an "Iron Curtain" of repression across Central Europe while America embarked on a strategy of containment of communism. Stopping the spread of communism in Asia was more problematic. Mao Zedong, a Chinese Communist, took over China in 1949, and in June 1950, Communist-supported North Korea invaded South Korea. The conflict was a frustrating, seesaw, three-year struggle.

Presidents Eisenhower and Kennedy continued containment with different military emphases. Both men also had trouble with the rise of Communism and Fidel Castro in Cuba. Vietnam became an increasing problem in the late 1950s, and by 1967, the U.S. had 540,000 troops in South Vietnam. The war ended badly in 1975 with a communist takeover of South Vietnam. By the late 1970s, America was frustrated and uncertain about its place in the world, eventually turning to Ronald Reagan, who promised to restore America's confidence and standing.

Domestically in 1945, Americans feared a return to depression. All of the post-war presidents accepted the basic government philosophy of the New Deal and maintained many of Roosevelt's programs. After President Kennedy's death in 1963, Lyndon Johnson had the most successful domestic presidential record since FDR. His Great Society program succeed in the areas of Civil Rights before the war in Vietnam consumed his administration

Ideas for Discussion

1. How did President Truman establish the cornerstones of American foreign policy for the next forty years?

2. Evaluate containment in Europe and in Asia from 1947 to 1955. What were its successes and failures?

3. Why didn't President Nixon tell the truth about Watergate?

Extend Your Understanding

For a complete review of Period 8: 1945–1980 and more Ideas for Discussion, scan the code or go to
www.sherpalearning.com/skillbook/review/unit-8

Prioritizing Facts
in Planning an Essay

The necessity of using relevant and appropriate evidence in your written arguments has been an overarching point throughout the lessons in this book. In previous sections, you examined how to support a thesis with factual information rather than generalities or opinions (Chapters

DISCIPLINARY PRACTICES
- **Analyzing Evidence**
- **Argument Development**

1, 22, 23). And elsewhere you also evaluated the relevancy of data in addressing a question (Chapter 8). This section will expand those ideas by considering how to prioritize facts when organizing your essay answer.

When you construct an answer, you probably cannot immediately arrange your facts in a logical and structured manner. Your first reaction should be to list as many facts about the topic as possible. After this initial brainstorming, you should begin to prioritize the information in terms of its usefulness and relevance to the topic.

In this section, you will work on establishing criteria for prioritizing facts. Clearly, not all material has the same importance in structuring your response. Depending on the focus of the prompt, you will need to rank information in terms of its effectiveness in proving your thesis. This process calls for establishing standards of significance, determining the utility of facts, and deciding which ones to highlight in the paper. Some data should be used first, other ideas will be useful later in the answer, and some evidence will be discarded completely.

As you prioritize facts, you should consider the following criteria:

1. Does a fact **directly address** the topic at hand? Does it deal with key elements of the question, including the correct chronological period? In other words, does it target the exact issue under consideration?

2. Does a fact deal with the **purpose** of the question? If the prompt concerns evaluating successes, do your facts deal with achievements and positive outcomes? If the prompt is about failure or setbacks, do the facts describe shortfalls or missed opportunities?

3. Does a fact deal with the **correct aspect** of the prompt? If a question asks about economic issues, is the evidence about monetary or financial issues? If the prompt asks about military matters, is a fact about strategy, troop morale, or battles?

4. Does a fact advance the **targeted Reasoning Skill** that is being assessed in the prompt? On the LEQ, you earn a point for correctly framing or structuring your argument according to the Reasoning Skill under consideration. For a comparison prompt, does the fact address a similarity or difference? For a causation prompt, does the fact help to establish a causal link to effects and results?

To summarize, the first priority is to use facts that are on the topic, deal with the correct time frame, and address the correct purpose/aspects of the question. Facts that have *some* of these elements are useful later in the paper, and those that have *none* of these characteristics should not be used at all. In the next part of the book, we will develop the idea of sequencing evidence, which is the flipside of prioritizing information.

Practicing the Skill

Directions: Below are three prompts about the Cold War and a list of possible facts that might be useful to answer them. First, look at the example question, the supporting facts, and the rationale for prioritizing the evidence from most useful (1) to irrelevant (4). After discussing the sample question and the rationale with your classmates, apply the skill with exercise questions 1 and 2.

Example Prompt: *How did events in Asia from 1949 to 1970 damage America's Cold War interest?*

Supporting Facts

___1___ Mao Zedong's victory in China

___4___ Building the Berlin Wall

___3___ The Korean conflict ended

___2___ The fall of Dien Bien Phu

All the events occurred during the period, yet Mao Zedong's victory was the most damaging to America's interest by establishing communism in the world's most populous nation. Next, the fall of Dien Bien Phu hurt the U.S. because it escalated America's role in Indochina and set the stage for the Vietnam debacle. Rather than a setback, the Korean conflict allowed the U.S. to claim a victory in containing communism. Finally, although the building of the Berlin Wall was a U.S. setback, it was not as damaging as the other issues, and it was a European event.

Applying the Skill

Directions: Prioritize the facts for these two questions, and write a brief rationale that explains your reasons for ranking the evidence as you did. Write your answers in your notebook.

Exercise Prompt 1: *How successful was President Dwight D. Eisenhower in containing communism in Europe between 1953 and 1961?*

Supporting Facts:

_____ The Geneva Conference of 1954

_____ Peaceful coexistence with the USSR

_____ The Hungarian uprising in 1956

_____ Strengthening NATO

Exercise Prompt 2: *Which of the following events was the most serious blow to America's international prestige in the Cold War?*

Supporting Facts

_____ The Cuban Missile Crisis

_____ The Camp David Accords

_____ The Bay of Pigs Invasion

_____ The Iran-Contra Affair

Sequencing Evidence in an Essay

In the previous section, you worked on prioritizing facts in planning an essay. Now we will look at a closely related aspect of that skill—sequencing evidence. The proper placement of information in your paper will add clarity to your thesis and make your point of view more persuasive.

DISCIPLINARY PRACTICES

- **Analyzing Evidence**
- **Argument Development**

Sequencing information requires you to use some of the same procedures that you employed in prioritizing facts. With both processes, you establish guidelines to decide which evidence to use first in your answer, which information should come next, and which data that should be discarded.

As you create the sequence for an argument, remember to consider the following:

1. **General statements first.** Always work from the general to the specific. Statements that provide an outline of the topic offer organization for supportive details and serve as topic sentences for the paragraph in your answer. A response that lays out your general point of view first leads effectively to the next step of adding specific support to prove your position.

2. **Facts before opinions.** As you know from previous chapters, the use of specific factual information is the key to convincing the reader of your position. Opinions may have a place in your paper, but only if they are extrapolated from facts. Generally they do not belong in an analytical essay and will carry little weight in a discussion.

3. **Statements that directly relate to the topic and the time period.** As has been emphasized throughout this book, specific, on-target facts are fundamental to proving your position.

4. **Statements that affirm your argument.** Always use evidence that supports your position first. Later in the essay, you may wish to insert rebuttal information in a concession paragraph. Including contrary information shows that you recognize the complexity of a historical problem, but it should never repudiate your thesis, nor should it appear too early in the paper. In an essay, you may acknowledge the other side of an issue, but only after completely presenting your supporting facts.

Practicing the Skill

Directions: Look at the following claim about Martin Luther King, Jr. and the Civil Rights Movement. Examine the claim, the point of view, and the proposed sequence of support for the various parts of the argument. Also analyze the rationale for their placement. Discuss the example with your classmates or members of your study group.

Claim: Martin Luther King, Jr. lost control of the Civil Rights Movement in the mid to late 1960s.

Point of View (Thesis): The rise of Black Nationalism and the lack of progress on racial equality put Martin Luther King, Jr. on the defensive between 1965 and 1968.

Put a 1 in front of the statement that you would use first, a 2 for the next statement that would follow, and so on.

   5   African Americans were unrealistic in the 1960s as they pushed too hard for equality.

   3   Malcolm X was a popular figure among young, urban blacks.

   2   The Black Panthers represented the frustration many African Americans felt about the slow pace of civil rights in the 1960s.

____1____ Many African Americans turned away from King's nonviolent, church-oriented approach to civil rights, and moved to a strategy of more direct action after 1965.

____4____ George Wallace represented a conservative reaction to the Civil Rights Movement in the late 1960s.

Rationale:

The statement about dissatisfaction with King's nonviolent approach is general but pertinent and could serve as an effective topic sentence. The statements about the Black Panthers and Malcolm X are useful to support the first statement. The George Wallace statement could be used in a concession paragraph. And the sentence about the unrealistic notion of equality is an opinion and should be discarded.

Applying the Skill

Directions: Now look at the claim about President Lyndon B. Johnson and civil rights. First, write a point of view, and then place the five potential statements of support into the most effective sequence. Next, provide a rationale for your decisions, using the exercise above as a model. Write your answers in your notebook.

Claim: President Lyndon Johnson was a great supporter of civil rights.

Point of View (Thesis):

Put a 1 in front of the statement that you would use first, a 2 for the next statement that would follow, and so on.

_____ In 1964, President Johnson got a landmark civil rights bill through Congress.

_____ President Kennedy did more for African Americans than Lyndon Johnson.

_____ President Johnson, as a southern conservative, surprised many African Americans with his strong advocacy of civil rights in the mid-1960s.

_____ The racial unrest of 1966–1967 tarnished President Johnson's accomplishments in civil rights.

_____ President Johnson appointed Thurgood Marshall, the first African American Supreme Court justice.

Rationale:

Steps for Writing a DBQ Essay

Throughout the book, you have examined various ideas and strategies that are helpful in planning and writing a DBQ essay. In this section, the steps for developing a DBQ response will be organized into a seven step program.

As you will see when we review the DBQ rubric in the last chapter, the analysis and application of documents is at the forefront of the redesigned DBQ. However, you should know that—in many ways—the DBQ and LEQ are similar. Both require a thesis that is supported by relevant evidence, and each essay requires that the prompt be put into a broader historical context. The major difference between the two questions is the need to integrate documents into your answer.

DISCIPLINARY PRACTICES
- **Analyzing Evidence**
- **Argument Development**

REASONING SKILLS
- **Causation**
- **Change over Time**
- **Comparison**
- **Contextualization**

Carefully read the **7 Steps for Writing a DBQ Essay** on the following page. In this chapter, you will practice applying the 7 Steps to a full-length DBQ question. You will also be introduced to the DBQ Planner Worksheet, which will guide you through the process of applying the 7 Steps to the DBQ provided.

7 Steps for Writing a DBQ Essay

Step 1: Read the prompt carefully—maybe as many as five times! Note the task and time period.

Step 2: If the prompt is a statement, rephrase the prompt into a question, or if the prompt is already in the form of a question, create a **clarifying question**.

Step 3: Answer the question you developed Step 2. This will serve as your **thesis statement**.

Step 4: Make a list of ALL information about the **time period** under consideration. Do this *before* looking at the documents. Don't be concerned that the information may later appear in the documents. These facts can be eliminated before you start to write your paper; initially "drain your brain."

Step 5: Analyze the sources. Determine each item's meaning, and then use **H.I.P.P.O.** to identify ONE aspect that you will discuss in your paper of at least 3 sources. Finally, use the **O.** part of **H.I.P.P.O.** to organize and apply at least 6 sources in support of your thesis.

Step 6: Put the documents and outside information into pro and con **categories** as they relate to your thesis.

Step 7: Provide **background** to the subject under consideration (contextualization).

Practicing the Skill

Directions: Begin by closely examining the DBQ prompt below, as well as the accompanying documents on the pages that follow.

The DBQ Planner Worksheet on page 150 will guide you with operationalizing the 7 Steps for planning and writing a DBQ essay. Several parts of the planner have been completed for the prompt below. Discuss the suggested responses with your group and how the planner is useful in constructing a DBQ response. If you are working independently, write your response in your notebook.

The following question is based on the accompanying documents. In your response you should do the following:

Thesis: Present a thesis that makes a defensible claim and responds to all parts of the question. It should not merely restate or rephrase the prompt, and should be placed either in the introduction or the conclusion.

Argument Development: Develop and support a cohesive argument that recognizes and accounts for historical complexity by explicitly illustrating relationships among historical evidence such as modification, corroboration, and/or qualification.

Use of Documents: Utilize the content of **at least six** documents to support the stated thesis or a relevant argument.

Sourcing the Documents: Explain the significance of the author's point of view, purpose, historical context, and/or audience for **at least three** documents.

Contextualization: Situate the argument by explaining the broader historical events, developments, or processes immediately relevant to the question.

Outside Information: Use **at least one** additional piece of specific historical evidence (beyond the documents) relevant to your argument.

Example Prompt: *Evaluate the changes in race relations in the United States from 1954–1964. Analyze the causes of these changes and the resistance to them.*

Document 1

Source: *Brown vs. Board of Education of Topeka*, May 1954

"We come then to the question presented: Does segregation of children in public schools solely on the basis of race, even though the physical facilities and other 'tangible' factors may be equal, deprive children of the minority group of equal educational opportunity? We believe it does…. We conclude that in the field of public education the doctrine of 'separate but equal' has no place…."

Document 2

Source: Mug Shot of Rosa Parks, December 1955

Document 3

Source: "A Southern Manifesto" signed by 101 Southern senators and representatives, March 1956

"We regard the decision of the Supreme Court in the school cases as a clear abuse of judicial power....The Supreme Court of the United States, with no legal basis for such action, undertook to exercise their naked judicial power and substituted their personal political and social ideas for the established law of the land....This unwarranted exercise of power by the Court,...is destroying the amicable relationship between the white and Negro races that have been created through 90 years of patient effort by the good people of both races...."

Document 4

Source: Letter from Governor Faubus of Arkansas to President Eisenhower, September 1957

"The question at issue at Little Rock this moment is not integration versus segregation....The question now is whether or not the head of a sovereign state can exercise his constitutional powers and discretion of maintaining peace and good order within his jurisdiction,...The situation... grows more explosive by the hour. This is caused for the most part by the misunderstanding of our problem by a federal judge who decreed 'immediate integration' of the public schools of Little Rock without hearing any evidence whatsoever as to the conditions now existing in the community...."

Document 5

Source: James Peck, *Freedom Ride*, May 1961

"Upon my arrival in Birmingham, I could see a mob lined up on the sidewalk only a few feet from the loading platform. Most of them were young—in their twenties. Some were carrying ill-concealed iron bars... All had hate showing on their faces....As we entered the white waiting room and approached the lunch counter, we were grabbed bodily and pushed toward the alleyway...six of them started swinging at me with fists and pipes....Within seconds, I was unconscious on the ground....When I regained consciousness, the alleyway was empty. Blood was flowing down my face...."

Document 6

Source: Excerpt of a speech by Martin Luther King, Jr. in Birmingham Alabama, April 1963

"I think I should indicate why I am here in Birmingham, since you have been influenced by the view which argues against 'outsiders coming in'... I cannot sit idly by in Atlanta and not be concerned about what happens in Birmingham. Injustice anywhere is a threat to justice everywhere.... For years now I have heard the word 'Wait!' It rings in the ear of every Negro with piercing familiarity. This 'Wait' has almost always meant 'Never.'... I submit that an individual who breaks a law that conscience tells him is unjust ... is in reality expressing the highest respect for the law."

Document 7

Source: "Looking back on it now, would you say that you approve or disapprove of the civil rights bill that was passed by Congress last month?" Harris Survey, August 1964

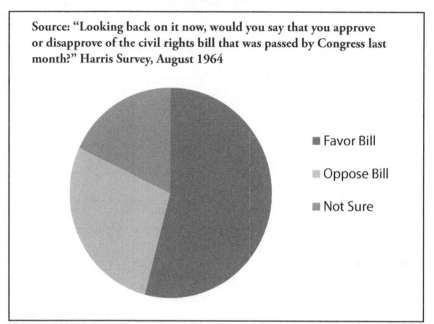

Applying the Skill

Directions: After you have finished reviewing and discussing the suggested responses provided in the DBQ Planner Worksheet on the pages that follow, use the worksheet to plan a complete response to the prompt above.

Copy the planner into your notebook, or print out a blank DBQ Planner Worksheet from the *U.S. History Skillbook* companion website (see page *xiv* for more information on accessing the companion website).

DBQ Planner Worksheet

Step 1 – Task Analyze the causes of the Civil Rights movement
and the resistance to it

Time Period 1950s and early 1960s

Step 2 – Clarifying Question _____

_____

_____

_____

Step 3 – Thesis _____

_____

_____

_____

Step 4 – Outside Information

Earl Warren's Court   Lyndon Johnson

_____   _____

E. D. Nixon   _____

_____   _____

_____   Civil Rights Act of 1957

_____   _____

_____   _____

Step 5 – Document Analysis (H.I.P.P.O.)

(use the chart on p. 152)

Step 6 – Pro and Con Categories

Pro	Con
Document 1	Document 3

Step 7 – Background (Contextualization)   The Civil Rights movement of the 1950s and 1960s had its antecedents going back to the end of World War II. The war effort of African Americans motivated the Truman administration to propose a civil rights plan in 1948. In addition, the National Association of Colored People won a series of Supreme Court cases that paved the way for the Warren's Court overturning of the 1896 case of *Plessy v. Ferguson* in 1954.

Doc.	H	I	P	P	O	Meaning
1	SC overturned the 1896 ruling that "separate but equal" facilities were Constitutional	The American people and the Congress of the United States			Ruling set the stage for the Civil Rights Revolution in the 1950s and 1960s	Schools and other aspects of American life must begin to integrate
2						
3						
4						
5						
6						
7						

Steps for Writing an LEQ Essay

Throughout this book, you have explored specific skills and strategies to facilitate the planning and writing of a full-length response to a Long Essay Question (LEQ) prompt. In this section, those elements are reviewed and summarized into a concise outline.

Before you can begin applying the 9 Steps to the LEQ prompt on the exam, you must choose a prompt from among the three provided. You will want to choose quickly so you can maximize your time for planning and writing. To help with your choice, keep the following in mind:

DISCIPLINARY PRACTICES
- **Analyzing Evidence**
- **Argument Development**

REASONING SKILLS
- **Causation**
- **Change over Time**
- **Comparison**
- **Contextualization**

1. The three prompts will address the same theme and reasoning skill.

2. There will be one question dealing with periods 1–3; one from periods 4–6; and one from periods 7–9.

3. Generally, you will know the most about prompts from your most recent classroom instruction—that is periods 7–9 or periods 4–6.

4. List all the facts you know about the topics and terms in each of the three prompts, and then choose the prompt with the longest, most detailed list. Use this list for Step 3 in the LEQ Planner Worksheet.

9 Steps for Writing an LEQ Essay

Step 1: Identify the critical words in the prompt that indicate

- the Reasoning Skill that is being targeted—comparison, causation, or continuity/change over time (note that contextualization will not be a targeted Reasoning Skill on the exam);
- the time period;
- the type of content appropriate as supportive information (e.g., political, social, economic, cultural, intellectual, chronological periods, and geographic areas).

Step 2: If the prompt is a statement, turn it into a clarifying question. If it is already a question, try rephrasing the question to distill it down further.

Step 3: Make a list of all of the facts you know related to the subject of the prompt.

Step 4: Write a strong thesis statement that

- makes a historically defensible claim;
- deals with all aspects of the topic;
- provides an organizational framework;
- addresses the core issues;
- may be positive, negative, or a combination of both.

Step 5: Organize the facts into categories, such as

- political, economic, and social (always good bets);
- chronological periods;
- geographic areas.

Step 6: In planning your answer, be sure to completely address all aspects of the prompt by

- dealing with all topics suggested;
- examining the entire chronological period mentioned;
- both describing as well as explaining the targeted skill.

Step 7: Write a strong introductory paragraph that contains

- a thesis;
- a general description of the topics to be addressed in the essay;
- a definition of important terms (if necessary);
- a transitional sentence that links the opening to the body of the paper.

Step 8: Develop paragraphs—each with topic sentences—that support the thesis.

Step 9: Write a concluding paragraph that

- summarizes the thesis;
- reviews the significant points from the body of the essay.

Considering the steps above, determine which step poses the most difficulty for you. Write the step you choose in your notebook, and make a note of any confusion you may have about the step. Next, refer to the sections of this book that address the skills and tasks that correspond to the step you chose as your "pain point." Discuss the nine steps and your response to the task above with your classmates or with the members of your study group.

Practicing the Skill

Directions: On the pages that follow, you will find an LEQ Planner Worksheet that will help you to operationalize the 9 Steps for Writing an LEQ Essay. In order to practice using the LEQ Planner Worksheet, begin by analyzing the following prompt:

Example Prompt: *Evaluate the extent to which the United States was successful in blocking Soviet expansion in Europe and Asia from 1947–1961.*

Several parts of the planner have been completed for the prompt above. Examine the sample responses in the planner, and then discuss—or take notes about—how the LEQ Planner Worksheet is useful in constructing an LEQ response. Knowing how the planner will benefit you will help you to use it more efficiently.

LEQ Planner Worksheet

Step 1 – Reasoning Skill _____

    Time Period _1943 to 1961_ (include 1943 to contextualize the origins of the Cold War.)

    Content Areas _____

Step 2 – Clarifying Question _How effective was the United States in_ _containing Soviet expansion in the earlier days of the Cold War?_

_____

_____

_____

Step 3 – The Facts I Know

Yalta Agreement	_____
Marshall Plan	_____
George Marshall	_____
_____	massive retaliation
_____	roll back communism
_____	_____
_____	_____
Chiang Kai Shek	_____
Fall of China	_____
_____	containment
Mao Tse Tung	_____
_____	_____
_____	_____
_____	_____

Step 4 – Thesis The United States was only partially successful in blocking Soviet expansion after World War II. They defended capitalism and democracy well in Europe, but experienced major setbacks in Asia.

Step 5 – Categories of Facts (from Step 3)

Europe	Asia
- Marshall Plan	- Fall of China
- containment	-
-	- Mao Tse Tung
-	-
- George Marshall	-
-	- Chiang Kai Shek
-	-
- massive retaliation	-
-	-
- roll back communism	-
- Yalta Agreement	-
-	-
-	-

Step 6 – Address the Prompt

Be sure the answer you have planned does the following:

☐ Deals with all topics/geographic areas

☐ Examines the entire chronological period

☐ Both describes and explains the targeted Reasoning Skill

Step 7 – Introductory Paragraph (begin with thesis from Step 4)

   a. General Development of Thesis _____

_____

_____

   b. Transitional Sentence   _A review of events from 1943–1961_

   will demonstrate the mixed results the United States had in

   blocking Soviet expansion in the early Cold War years.

Step 8 – Supporting Paragraphs

   Topic Sentence (Para 1) _____

_____

_____

   Topic Sentence (Para 2) _____

_____

_____

   Topic Sentence (Para 3) _____

_____

_____

Step 9 – Concluding Paragraph

   a. Summary of Thesis _____

_____

_____

   b. General Review of Argument _____

_____

_____

Applying the Skill

Directions: Now complete the blank sections of the planner for the Cold War prompt on page 156.

Copy the planner on the preceding pages into your notebook, or print out a blank LEQ Planner Worksheet from the *U.S. History Skillbook* companion website (see page *xiv* for more information on accessing the companion website).

When you have finished filling in the planner, discuss how and why you developed the various sections of the worksheet as you did.

Unit 9

America Redefined

Barack Obama is sworn in as the 44th president, January 20, 2009
— photo by Master Sgt. Cecilio Ricardo, U.S. Air Force

Period 9: 1980–Present

Period Summary

Ronald Reagan promised a new direction for America in 1981. He began what some called the "Reagan Revolution." He cut social spending, reduced income taxes 30 percent, and embarked on a massive military buildup to confront the USSR.

In 1988, George H.W. Bush was elected to what some called "Reagan's third term." Bush organized a multi-national force that drove Iraq from Kuwait and restored stability in the region. While his popularity soared after this success, it quickly plummeted as the nation slipped into a deep recession, costing him reelection in 1992.

Bill Clinton's presidency was dogged by charges of political and personal scandal, and in his second term he was accused of sexual misconduct, culminating in his impeachment and acquittal by the Senate.

Though George W. Bush entered office under a cloud after the controversial election in 2000, his presidency was quickly transformed by the September 11th terrorist attacks. Bush declared a war on terrorism and the U.S. attacked Afghanistan and Iraq. The United States quickly deposed Saddam Hussein, but an uncontrolled civil war broke out in Iraq, which eroded the president's support as the invasion devolved into a quagmire.

In 2008, after eight years of Republican rule, with the nation despairing over the economy and the war against terror, Barack Obama became the nation's first African-American president. This historic event was heralded by great hope for a change in the direction of the country.

Ideas for Discussion

1. Ronald Reagan ended the Cold War. Evaluate this statement.

2. How did 9/11 mark a turning point in American history?

3. What did the election of Barack Obama say about American's view of themselves and their nation?

Extend Your Understanding

For a complete review of Period 9: 1980–Present and more Ideas for Discussion, scan the code or go to
www.sherpalearning.com/skillbook/review/unit-9

A Review of the Disciplinary Practices and Reasoning Skills

In this book, you have been introduced to and worked on the two Disciplinary Practices and four Reasoning Skills that define the foundations of the redesigned AP United States History curriculum. In this section, you will find a review of these practices and skills with references to where they are addressed in the text.

The AP History Disciplinary Practices

#1.   Analyzing Historical Evidence (Primary and Secondary Sources)— The ability to weigh, analyze, and evaluate evidence from a variety of sources and to use them effectively in a historical argument. (Units 1–9)

#2.   Argument Development—The ability to define and frame a question about the past, and to construct a written response to that problem using a historically defensible claim (thesis) and supporting it with specific and relevant evidence. (Units 1–9)

The AP History Reasoning Skills

#1.   Causation—The ability to identify, analyze, and evaluate what caused certain events to occur, and the nature of cause-and-effect relationships in history. Also, to differentiate between primary and secondary causes and short- and long-term effects. (Units 2, 3)

#2. **Continuity and Change over Time**—The ability to describe and explain patterns of continuity and change over time. Also, the ability to evaluate how events contributed to maintaining the status quo yet fostered change over time. (Units 1, 5, 7, 9)

#3. **Comparison**—The ability to understand and explain the similarities and differences between two (or more) developments and/or phenomena. (Units 5, 9)

#4. **Contextualization**—The ability to connect the events in a time period with other larger processes or phenomena in another time and place—often as background information (setting the scene) for the development of an argument. And to explain how this different setting may have influenced the topic under consideration. (Units 4, 5, 6, 8)

Applying the Skill

Directions: As you examine the Disciplinary Practices and Reasoning Skills summaries above, consider the following questions about their application in your study of history. Write your responses in your notebook, and then discuss them with your classmates or study group.

1. Why is contextualization included as an important skill in studying and writing history?

2. What aspects of developing an argument is most challenging for you as you construct your essay responses?

3. Do you think the ability to analyze historical evidence is the most important skill in studying history? If so, why?

4. To what degree is there a danger in establishing cause-and-effect relationships too quickly as you study historical events?

5. In what ways are comparison and contextualization related to each other in the study of history?

6. Educational Testing Service® has identified four main reasoning skills as the core of historical thinking. Would you suggest additional skills for your personal study of AP United States History?

Writing a DBQ Essay

The DBQ is a critical element of the AP course and on the exam. The question is required for all test-takers and calls for specific skills in its mastery. Throughout the book, you have built the skills necessary for writing this type of essay. Now it is time to apply them all as you compose a DBQ essay response.

DISCIPLINARY PRACTICES

- **Analyzing Evidence**
- **Argument Development**

REASONING SKILLS

- **Causation**
- **Change over Time**
- **Comparison**
- **Contextualization**

Practicing the Skill

Directions: In Unit 8, you examined the steps necessary for writing a complete DBQ. In your notebook, recreate the list in abbreviated form. You may want to try to recreate the list from memory before returning to the list on page 144.

When you have finished reviewing the steps, write a rationale for the element(s) of the writing process you consider to be the most significant. Limit your response to one or two sentences. Next, list a few notes on how the DBQ essay is similar yet different from the LEQ essay. Discuss your responses with your classmates or the members of your study group.

Applying the Skill

Directions: Below is a Document-Based Question about the 1960s. Using the planning techniques discussed in the previous unit, write an essay response to the prompt. A blank DBQ Planner Worksheet begins on page 172. You may also print a blank worksheet template from the companion website (see page 177 for details about accessing the worksheet templates).

As this is your first time using the DBQ Planner Worksheet without the help of any suggested responses, and perhaps your first attempt at a complete DBQ response, you should take your time and carefully address each step. Note, however, that under testing conditions you would allow yourself 15 minutes for preparation and 45 minutes to write.

The following question is based on the accompanying documents. In your response you should do the following:

Thesis: Present a thesis that makes a defensible claim and responds to all parts of the question. It should not merely restate or rephrase the prompt, and should be placed either in the introduction or the conclusion.

Argument Development: Develop and support a cohesive argument that recognizes and accounts for historical complexity by explicitly illustrating relationships among historical evidence such as modification, corroboration, and/or qualification.

Use of Documents: Utilize the content of **at least six** documents to support the stated thesis or a relevant argument.

Sourcing the Documents: Explain the significance of the author's point of view, purpose, historical context, and/or audience for **at least three** documents

Contextualization: Situate the argument by explaining the broader historical events, developments, or processes immediately relevant to the question.

Outside Information: Use **at least one** additional piece of specific historical evidence (beyond the documents) relevant to your argument.

Exercise Question: *Evaluate the extent to which the conflict over Vietnam changed American political and social beliefs in the 1960s.*

Document 1

Source: Bill Mauldin, "The Strategists," *The Sun-Times* (Chicago), 1966

Document 2

Source: Dean Rusk and Robert McNamara's Report to President Kennedy, November 11, 1961

The deteriorating situation in South Viet-Nam requires attention to the nature and scope of the United States national interests in that country. The loss of South Viet-Nam to Communism would involve the transfer of a nation of 20 million people from the free world to the Communism block. The loss of South Viet-Nam would make pointless any further discussion about the importance of Southeast Asia to the free world. ... The United States should commit itself to the clear objective of preventing the fall of South Viet-Nam to Communist [sic]. ... We should be prepared to introduce United States combat forces if that should become necessary for success. Dependent upon the circumstances, it may also be necessary for United States forces to strike at the source of the aggression in North Viet-Nam.

Document 3

Source: Tom Hayden, *Port Huron Statement*, June 1962

Unlike youth in other countries we are used to moral leadership being exercised and moral dimensions being clarified by our elders. But today, for us, not even the liberal and socialist preachments of the past seem adequate to the forms of the present ... We oppose the depersonalization that reduces human beings to the status of things. ... As a social system we seek the establishment of a democracy of individual participation, governed by two central aims: that the individual share in those social decisions determining the quality and direction of life, that society be organized to encourage independence in men and provide the media for their common participation.

It is imperative that the means of violence be abolished and the institutions—local, national, international—that encourage non-violence as a condition of conflict be developed. [Thousands of students] move actively and directly against racial injustices, the threat of war, violations of the individual rights of conscience, and, less frequently, against economic manipulation... .

Document 4

Source: Dr. Martin Luther King, Jr., speech in New York City, April 4, 1967

A few years ago there was a shining moment… . It seemed as if there was a real promise of hope for the poor—both black and white—through the poverty program. There were experiments, hopes, new beginnings. Then came the buildup in Vietnam and I watched the program broken and eviscerated as if it were some idle political plaything of a society gone mad about war, and I knew that America would never invest the necessary funds or energies in rehabilitation of its poor so long as adventures like Vietnam continued to draw men and skills and money … So I was increasingly compelled to see the war as an enemy of the poor and to attack it as such … it became clear to me that the war was doing far more than devastating the hopes of the poor at home. It was sending their sons and their brothers and their husbands to fight and to die in extraordinary high proportions relative to the rest of the population… .

Document 5

Source: Vietnam War protesters outside the White House, January 19, 1968

Document 6

Source: *Historical Statistics of the United States, Colonial Times to 1970*

Outlays of the Federal Government by Major Functions
1961–1970 (in millions)

Year	Total Outlays	Defense	(% of Total)	Health	(%)	Education	(%)
1961	97.7	47.3	48.4%	.8	.8%	1.2	1.0%
1962	106.8	51.0	47.7	1.1	1.0	1.4	1.3
1963	111.3	52.5	47.1	1.3	1.1	1.5	1.3
1964	118.5	53.5	45.1	1.7	1.4	1.7	1.4
1965	118.4	49.5	41.8	1.7	1.4	2.2	1.8
1966	134.6	56.7	42.1	2.5	1.8	4.2	3.1
1967	158.5	70.0	44.2	6.6	4.1	5.8	3.6
1968	178.8	80.5	45.0	9.6	5.3	6.7	3.7
1969	184.5	81.2	44.0	11.6	6.2	6.5	3.5
1970	196.5	80.2	41.0	12.9	6.5	7.2	3.6

Document 7

Source: Excerpt, "Self-Portrait of a Child of Amerika," Jerry Rubin, 1970

I am a child of Amerika …

I dodged the draft.

I went to Oberlin College for a year, graduated from the University of Cincinnati, spent 1 ½ years in Israel and started graduate school at Berkeley

I dropped out.

I dropped out of the White Race and the Amerikan nation.

I dig being free.

I like getting high.

I don't own a suit or tie.

I live for the revolution.

I'm a yippie.

I am an orphan of Amerika.

★ DBQ Planner Worksheet

Step 1 – Task _____

_____

Time Period _____

Step 2 – Clarifying Question _____

_____

_____

_____

Step 3 – Thesis _____

_____

_____

_____

Step 4 – Outside Information

_____   _____

_____   _____

_____   _____

_____   _____

_____   _____

_____   _____

Step 5 – Document Analysis (H.I.P.P.O.)

(use the chart on p. 174)

Step 6 – Pro and Con Categories

Pro	Con

Step 7 – Background (Contextualization) _____

_____

_____

_____

_____

_____

_____

_____

_____

Doc.	H.	I.	P.	P.	O.	Meaning
1						
2						
3						
4						
5						
6						
7						

Writing an LEQ Essay

The skills necessary for writing an essay response to a Long Essay Question prompt have been highlighted throughout this text and were summarized in Chapter 33. In this section, you will put all of those skills to use as you write an LEQ essay. As you complete your preparation for the final exam in your AP class (and for the actual AP U.S. History exam in May), you should practice writing LEQ essays by reviewing and applying the organizational system presented in Unit 8 to practice questions, like those found throughout this text or on the companion website.

DISCIPLINARY PRACTICES
- **Analyzing Evidence**
- **Argument Development**

REASONING SKILLS
- **Causation**
- **Change over Time**
- **Comparison**
- **Contextualization**

Practicing the Skill

Directions: Before you begin to write a full-length response to an LEQ prompt, review the **9 Steps for Writing an LEQ Essay**. As you did for the DBQ in the previous chapter, see how many of the steps you can recall from memory before reviewing the list on pages 154–155.

After reviewing the list, discuss the 9 Steps with your classmates or your study group. Evaluating your understanding of the process and discussing it with others will help you to identify your strengths and weaknesses in planning and completing this type of essay.

Applying the Skill

Directions: Below are three prompts about United States history from periods 1–3, 4–6, and 7–9 in the AP curriculum. You will see that each question focuses on the same Reasoning Skill (in this instance, Continuity and Change over Time), which is the format of the LEQs on the exam. Select one of the three prompts and write a complete essay response. Use the LEQ Planner Worksheet and the strategies discussed earlier in the book, and try to compose your answer in **40 minutes**—the recommended time for an LEQ response on the AP exam.

Exercise Question 1: *Evaluate the extent to which the American Revolution contributed to maintaining continuity as well as fostered change in America's political, social, and economic relationships from 1776–1789.*

Exercise Question 2: *Evaluate the extent to which the demand for currency reform contributed to maintaining continuity as well as fostered change in America from 1870–1900.*

Exercise Question 3: *Evaluate the extent to which the presidency of Ronald Reagan contributed to maintaining continuity as well as fostered change in America during the 1980s and beyond.*

Copy the LEQ Planner Worksheet that begins on the following page into your notebook. Copying the planner by hand may seem tedious, but it will help you to commit the steps to memory.

You can also download and print a blank LEQ Planner Worksheet from the *U.S. History Skillbook* companion website. To go directly to the collection of printable worksheets, point your browser to the following address:

https://www.sherpalearning.com/skillbook/worksheets

 If you're able to view and print PDF files from your phone or tablet, just scan this QR code with your device's camera.

★ LEQ Planner Worksheet

Step 1 – Reasoning Skill _____

    Time Period _____

    Content Areas _____

Step 2 – Clarifying Question _____

_____

_____

_____

Step 3 – The Facts I Know

_____   _____

_____   _____

_____   _____

_____   _____

_____   _____

_____   _____

_____   _____

_____   _____

_____   _____

_____   _____

_____   _____

_____   _____

Step 4 – Thesis _____

_____

_____

_____

Step 5 – Categories of Facts (from Step 3)

Step 6 – Address the Prompt

Be sure the answer you have planned does the following:

❑ Deals with all topics/geographic areas

❑ Examines the entire chronological period

❑ Both describes and explains the targeted Reasoning Skill

Step 7 – Introductory Paragraph (begin with thesis from Step 4)

   a. General Development of Thesis _____

_____

_____

   b. Transitional Sentence _____

_____

_____

Step 8 – Supporting Paragraphs

   Topic Sentence (Para 1) _____

_____

_____

   Topic Sentence (Para 2) _____

_____

_____

   Topic Sentence (Para 3) _____

_____

_____

Step 9 – Concluding Paragraph

   a. Summary of Thesis _____

_____

_____

   b. General Review of Argument _____

_____

_____

Understanding the DBQ and LEQ Rubrics

In order to ensure validity and reliability in the grading of essays, your teacher will use a rubric to evaluate your writing. By understanding the elements of a rubric, how it is constructed, and how it is used in the grading process, you will gain important insights into the standards of excellence expected on the test, thereby enhancing your performance on the writing section of the exam. Through an appreciation of the specifics of rubric construction, you will discover what exactly exam readers look for as they evaluate student essay responses.

Practicing the Skill

Directions: The College Board® recently published revised rubrics for both the DBQ and LEQ. The new rubrics are available on AP Central. To access them you should follow the navigation directions on the following page, or simply scan the QR code with your phone or tablet. While the location of the rubrics may change over time, the QR code will be continually updated to point to the new location.

After you have downloaded or printed the rubrics, discuss your understanding of their meaning with your classmates or study group. If you are working alone, write down a few thoughts about the rubrics before moving on to the Applying the Skill section. Remember, it's important to understand how to structure your essays to conform to the rubrics in order to ensure that you earn the highest score for your work.

Accessing the 2018 Rubrics

1. Point your browser to the *U.S. History Skillbook* companion website: **https://www.sherpalearning.com/skillbook**

2. Look for the "LINKS & OTHER RESOURCES" box in the selection of resource categories below the welcome message. Click on it.

3. In the section called "LINKS TO VITAL COURSE INFO," click on "**The Revised Rubrics for the 2018 Exam**" to go directly to the printable PDF on the AP Central™ website.

4. The new rubrics can be found on pages 2 & 3 of the PDF.

    To view the PDF on your phone or tablet, simply point your device's camera at the QR code.

Applying the Skill

Directions: A rubric lists "what counts" in an essay answer. It defines performance expectations and cites the most important components of a superior response to a DBQ or LEQ essay prompt. By analyzing the rubric scoring process, you answer the question: *What do I need to do to receive a high score on an exam essay?*

The **Rubric Guides** presented on pages 185 and 188 will help to simplify the rubrics and make them more user-friendly. Use the first part of each rubric guide to review your DBQ and LEQ essays from the previous chapters. By using the rubrics to evaluate your own responses, you will train yourself to recognize the elements of a high-scoring essay, and how you can integrate those elements into your responses.

Looking at the **Rubric Guide** on page 185, you can see the seven point rubric is divided into four general areas. As you examine each part of the rubric, you should look back at the various chapters in the book that address each component.

A THESIS/CLAIM

In Chapters 16 and 18, you were introduced to the elements of a strong thesis (**The A.C.I.D. Test**) and the various possible types of thesis statements.

Hints & Tips

- Do more than restate the question
- Take a clear position
- Put your thesis in the first paragraph

B CONTEXTUALIZATION

In Chapters 17, 19, 21, 24, and 28, you dealt with establishing contextualization in your essay and how documents, charts, and cartoons could be used to provide a context to your argument.

Hints & Tips

- Use more than a phrase or sentence
- "Set the stage" in the first paragraph
- Using prior events to contextualize is a good bet

C EVIDENCE

In Chapters 5, 8,14, 15, 21, 24 and 27, you worked with activities to analyze historical context (situation), intended audience, point of view, purpose, and organizing/using documents in support of an argument (**H.I.P.P.O.**). Specifically, you practiced using documents to support an argument (the O in H.I.P.P.O.). Finally, you were introduced to determining relevant outside information and its placement in a historical argument (Chapters 1, 9, 22, 23, 30, and 31).

Hints & Tips

- Use several pieces of evidence
- List outside evidence before looking at the documents
- Use the documents as <u>support</u> of your argument
- Use all of the documents
- Don't summarize the documents

D   ANALYSIS AND REASONING

In Chapters 5, 8, 14, 15, 21, 24, 25, and 27, you dealt with establishing how and why documents were relevant to an argument. And, in other parts of the book, you had an opportunity to demonstrate a more complex understanding of historical development by analyzing cause and effect, assessing similarities and differences, explaining change over time, and dealing with diverse or alternative views of evidence (Chapters 3, 7, 15, and 25).

Hints & Tips

- Use all of the documents
- Employ **H.I.P.P.O.**
- Draw warranted conclusions by:
    - ⇨ establishing similarities and differences, **OR**
    - ⇨ developing cause and effect, **OR**
    - ⇨ connecting events across time periods, **OR**
    - ⇨ establishing alternative views about the prompt

★ DBQ Rubric Guide

A	**Thesis/Claim** (1 point)	1 point for presenting a thesis that makes a historically defensible claim and addresses all parts of the question
B	**Contextualization** (1 point)	1 point for describing a broader historical context relevant to the prompt
C	**Evidence** (3 points)	**Evidence from the Documents**
		1 point for using the content of at least **3 documents** to address the topic of the prompt **OR** 2 points for supporting an argument in response to the prompt using at least **6 documents**
		Evidence *beyond* the Documents
		1 point for using at least **1 additional piece of the specific historical evidence** (beyond that found in the documents) relevant to an argument about the prompt
D	**Analysis and Reasoning** (2 points)	1 point for explaining how or why a document's point of view, purpose, or historical situation, or audience is relevant to an argument—for at least **3 documents**
		1 point for demonstrating a complex understanding of the historical development that is the focus of the prompt, using evidence to corroborate, qualify, or modify an argument that addresses the question

Updated to reflect most recent changes from the College Board®—August 2017

Looking at the LEQ rubric on page 188, you can see it has six points divided into four categories. The first two reporting categories are the same as for the DBQ. Sections C and D, however, vary slightly from the DBQ rubric because this type of essay does not include documents. The skills necessary to earn the all of these points are covered in earlier parts of this book.

A THESIS/CLAIM

In Chapters 16 and 18, you were introduced to the elements of a strong thesis (**The A.C.I.D. Test**) and the various possible types of thesis statements.

Hints & Tips

- Do more than restate the question
- Take a clear position
- Put thesis in first paragraph

B CONTEXTUALIZATION

In Chapters 17, 19, 21, 24, and 28, you dealt with establishing contextualization in your essay.

Hints & Tips

- Use more than a phrase or sentence
- "Set the stage" in the first paragraph
- Using prior events to contextualize is a good bet

C EVIDENCE

In Chapters 1, 4, 7, 9, 22, 23, 25, 30, and 31, you worked on identifying and using specific evidence to support an argument.

Hints & Tips

- Use SPECIFIC, RELEVANT information
- Avoid generalizations

D   ANALYSIS AND REASONING

In Chapters 3, 4, 7, 20, 21, and 27, you were introduced to various historical reasoning skills, and in Chapters 3, 7, 15, and 25, you had an opportunity to demonstrate a more complex understanding of historical developments by analyzing cause and effect, assessing similarities and differences, explaining change over time, and dealing with diverse or alternative views of evidence.

Hints & Tips

- Make clear the reasoning skill to be addressed
- Draw warranted conclusions by:
    - ⇨ establishing similarities and differences, **OR**
    - ⇨ developing cause and effect, **OR**
    - ⇨ connecting events across time periods, **OR**
    - ⇨ establishing alternative views about the prompt

★ LEQ Rubric Guide

A	**Thesis/Claim** (1 point)	1 point for responding to the prompt with a historically defensible thesis/claim that establishes a line of reasoning		
B	**Contextualization** (1 point)	1 point for describing a broader historical context relevant to the prompt		
C	**Evidence** (2 points)	1 point for providing specific examples of evidence relevant to the topic of the prompt	OR	2 points for supporting an argument in response to the prompt using specific relevant examples of evidence
D	**Analysis and Reasoning** (2 points)	1 point for using historical reasoning (e.g., Comparison, Causation, Continuity/Change over Time) to frame or structure an argument that addresses the prompt	OR	2 points for demonstrating a complex understanding of the historical development that is the focus of the prompt, using evidence to corroborate, qualify or modify an argument that addresses the prompt

Updated to reflect most recent changes from the College Board®—August 2017

Appendices

Appendix

A

About the
AP U.S. History Course

Introduction to Advanced Placement

The Advanced Placement program is an educational testing program that offers college-level curricula to secondary school students. It is based on a fundamental premise: motivated high school students are capable of doing college-level work while still attending high school. The program also supports the belief that students are not being sufficiently challenged academically, especially in their last years of high school.

Advanced Placement (AP) officially started in 1955. Beginning with 11 subjects (U. S. History was not one of the originals), 1229 students took the first AP tests in May 1956. In 2014 there were thirty-seven AP courses offered, and students took more than 4.1 million examinations worldwide. Today, over 60% of American high schools offer at least one AP course.

The exams are constructed and administered by Educational Testing Service (ETS) under the aegis of the College Board®. The exams define the knowledge and skills of a freshman-level college course. Students who qualify on the exam (scoring three or better on a five-point scale) are recommended for college credit and placement. The final decision on awarding credit or placement rests with the college or university that the test-taker plans to attend, however. The College Board® reports the scores and makes it recommendations, but the Board cannot offer college credit or placement itself.

AP is now more than sixty years old and has become a standard of excellence in American secondary education. Throughout the United States—and even worldwide—AP has become synonymous with academic excellence and is regarded as an opportunity for high school students to dramatically expand their knowledge and skills.

The Benefits of an AP Course

AP classes offer students many benefits and opportunities. First, and most importantly, AP is an outstanding educational program that introduces college courses into high schools. Students receive instruction in content and skill development that they would normally receive only in their first year of college. AP courses go into greater depth and detail than regular high school courses as they offer more stimulating and challenging curricula. In short, AP provides high school students with a superior academic experience.

Other benefits include the following:

- By qualifying on the end-of-the-year exam, students can receive college credit and placement while still in high school.

- With sufficient numbers of AP courses and qualifying scores, students can earn sophomore standing at over fourteen hundred colleges and universities. This can result in substantial tuition savings. (Parents tend to appreciate this one.)

- Students can exempt introductory college courses and begin studying in their major field of interest earlier and/or they can explore other academic areas of interest.

- On a transcript, AP courses serve as an indicator to college admission officers that students are dedicated and willing to accept challenges in their education.

- AP courses provide students with a national standard by which to measure their academic progress.

- AP offers the opportunity for self-discovery. Through the AP challenge, students can better define their scholarly strengths and weaknesses and see themselves more clearly in comparison to other students around the country and the world.

What to Expect in AP U.S. History

An AP U.S. History class is an intensive study of the history of the United States from 1491 to the present. It makes the same academic demands that both parts of a college survey class would involve.

In general, you will be asked to:

- read 30 to 60 pages from a college-level, history textbook per week;

- outline or take reading notes from the textbook assignments;

- establish relationships among facts and be able to formulate concepts and generalizations about events, people, and ideas in American history;

- take notes from classroom lectures;

- participate in class discussions about various historical topics;

- understand and analyze primary sources including documents, cartoons, charts, and graphs;

- think historically—that is, analyze evidence, causation, and change over time; make comparisons; establish contextualization; provide interpretation; and create written arguments;

- write coherent, persuasive analytical essay answers about historical problems;

- utilize primary source materials along with relevant outside information to write analytical essays about historical problems.

How to Succeed in AP U.S. History

A simple truth exists about AP U.S. History: There are no shortcuts or "magic bullets" that lead to a good grade or qualifying score on the test. In order to succeed, a student must commit to a year-long protocol of nightly study, periodic review, and intense application of the content and skills taught in the course.

The most important path to success is to stay current with the reading and complete all assignments in a timely fashion. Cramming will not work in AP United States History. You should allocate at least one to two hours of preparation for your AP history class per night.

On a regular basis, you must write in-class essays on significant history problems. In addition, you must write document-based essays. All writing must have a strong thesis that is thoughtfully developed and defended. Students must heed the advice of their teacher to improve and strengthen their writing skills.

A consistent and regular review schedule should be established. You should periodically look back on previous materials and relate them to current classroom work. The creation of outlines, charts, and other graphic organizers is an excellent means of review. Review of content should not be left until the end of the year, as the exam approaches. It must be a regular weekly or biweekly activity during the year. The formation of a study group is an excellent means to structure a review program. The group should meet at least once a month in the first semester and twice a month as the exam approaches.

About the AP U.S. History Exam

Overview of the Exam

The AP U.S. History Exam is 3 hours and 15 minutes long and is divided into two sections:

Section 1 (95 minutes): This section contains several sets of Multiple-Choice Questions (Part A) and three Short-Answer Questions (Part B).

Section 2 (100 minutes): Traditionally referred to as the "writing" portion of the exam, the second section includes the DBQ (Part A) and a choice of three LEQs (Part B).

Section	Part	Type of Question	# of Questions	Length of Time	% of Total Score
I	A	Multiple-Choice Questions	55	55 min	40%
	B	Short-Answer Questions	3	40 min	20%
II	A	Document-Based Question	1	60 min	25%
	B	Long Essay Questions	1 (of 3)	40 min	15%

Each part of the exam will be described in detail on the pages that follow.

Multiple-Choice Questions

Mastery of the multiple-choice section is critical to qualifying on the AP exam. The section consists of 55 items (49 are counted to calculate your score and six are piloted items to be used on future exams). This section counts for 40% of your overall grade. You will be asked to respond to stimulus materials such as documents, images, charts, graphs, or maps, and answer two to five questions about the source. The items are historically based and not designed to test your reading comprehension alone. You will need to demonstrate your reasoning abilities as well as your knowledge of history. Each item will have four answer choices consisting of one correct response and three distractors.

The multiple-choice questions will be arranged in sets of two to five items and will ask you to do the following:

- identify goals outlined in the source

- recognize long-term effects or results outlined in the source

- connect goals presented in one historical period with those in another

- relate the developments in a source to similar developments in another time period

- identify groups that would support the position expressed in a source

- identify groups that would oppose the position expressed in a source

- identify the influences at work on the author of a source

- analyze how a source serves as evidence for a specific development

- establish cause-and-effect relationships

- recognize how views expressed in a source reflected larger developments in another era

In general, if you answer 50-65% of the multiple-choice items correctly and do reasonably well on the essays, you have a high probability of qualifying for college credit. As an example, let's look at the average scores students earned on the 2017 exam.

Question Type	Avg. Score Earned	Total Points Available	Weighted Score
Multiple-Choice Questions	30.6	52	30.7
Short-Answer Questions	6.0	9	17.3
Document-Based Question	3.1	7	14.4
Long Essay Question	2.9	6	9.4
		Composite Score:	**71.8**

A student who earned the composite score of 71.8 would receive a 3 on the test. In order to earn the average score for multiple-choice shown above, a student would have to answer 59% of the multiple-choice questions correctly. That's 28.9 out of the 49 questions.

In the past, students have had to decide whether or not they should guess at answers for unanswered multiple-choice questions. However, due to recent changes in the scoring of the exam, this is no longer a factor. There is now no penalty for wrong answers. Since you cannot know which items are being piloted, the answer is undoubtedly, yes—**you should answer every question.** Whether you are certain about the answer or not, answer every question. That is the only way you can earn the maximum score.

Strategies for the Multiple-Choice Section

Here are a few tips on dealing with multiple-choice questions:

- Before looking at the source, read the stem of the question at least twice and identify the exact parameters of the task. In other words, determine what you are trying to determine. Assess the year, decade, or century of concern, and whether the question is asking about politics, economics, art, civil rights, etc.

- Next, go to the source and underline the main ideas of the document. Highlight material that directly relates to your task.

- If the source is a cartoon, graph, or map, don't forget to make use of the strategies you learned earlier in this book (see Units 4 & 5). They are effective tools when dealing with sources for any question type.

- Read all four choices before selecting the correct answer. Do not jump at the first answer that seems correct; you may find a better answer as you read through all the choices. You are looking for the BEST or MOST DIRECT answer.

While indiscriminate guessing is not a good idea, you should make educated guesses where you can on the test. That is, when the correct response is not a certainty and you do not want to leave the question blank, try to eliminate some of the distractors and then select from the remaining choices. For example, if you can reduce the four choices to two, you now have a 50% chance of answering correctly. Always start by eliminating wrong choices and then selecting from the remaining possibilities.

Here are a few tips for making educated guesses:

- First, eliminate choices that are outside the chronological period. For example, if the question deals with colonial religious development, a choice about George Washington's presidency would be the first to go.

- Next, eliminate choices that are wrong under any circumstances. If, in the example just cited, you see a choice about Alexander Hamilton's support of limiting the power of the government, that choice should be discarded.

- Finally, eliminate choices that do not address the topic of the question. For example, if a question topic concerns religious development, you can quickly eliminate choices about nullification, Social Darwinism, or other political and economic matters.

Once you have narrowed down the answer choices, it will be easier to select from the remaining options. Generally, your first choice is most likely correct. If you go back and change answers because you have some lingering doubt, you are very likely doing more harm than good.

Short-Answer Questions

Short-Answer Questions (SAQs) make up 20% of your score on the AP exam and require specific skills to answer effectively. Since the details of the course redesign were released back in 2014, this newer question type has caused quite a bit of stir. While the SAQ has not been the primary focus of this book, the skills you have learned will be invaluable.

There are four Short-Answer Questions on the test. The first two questions are both required, whereas you must choose between questions 3 and 4. The first SAQ will ask you to analyze a secondary source (see Chapters 11 and 26). Question 2 will assess the skills of Comparison or Causation, and will include a primary source text or a visual source, like a map, chart, or image. Questions 3 and 4 will assess whichever skill was not assessed in Question 2—Comparison or Causation. Questions 3 and 4 will *not* include a source. See the table below for an overview of the four Short-Answer Questions.

Question	Type	Source	Required	Possible Time Periods
1	Source Analysis	Secondary Source	Yes	Periods 3–8
2	Comparison or Causation	Primary/Visual Source	Yes	Periods 3–8
3	Comparison or Causation	None	Choose one	Periods 1–5
4		None		Periods 6–9

Strategies for the Short-Answer Questions

Here are several ideas to consider as you confront these questions:

- SAQs are not essay questions. Remember that the "SA" in SAQ stands for "short-answer." Do not write an essay. The question can be effectively answered with several sentences. The SAQ does not require the development and inclusion of a thesis statement.

- There will be three parts to each question, each worth 1 point. Your final score will be the average of your scores on each of the three questions answered.

- Your response should include specific facts that support your answer, not just opinions or generalities.

- Keep your answer contained within the allotted writing space provided in your answer book.

- You should label your answers a, b, and c to coincide with the three parts of the question. This is not required, but it will be helpful to you, as well as to those scoring your responses.

The Document-Based Question

Throughout this book you have been introduced to the skills necessary to successfully address the Document-Based Question (DBQ). It is required of every test-taker and counts as 25% of the overall score on the examination. The intent of the question is for you to formulate a thesis and support it with relevant evidence extracted from the seven documents provided. You must employ the historian's craft of sorting, weighing, and evaluating materials as you synthesize these sources into a coherent argument. The process calls for you to establish your position with a close analysis of documents, as well as with information not found in the seven sources provided. This outside information should be beyond the specific focus of the question and must be incorporated into your answer to earn the maximum number of points.

Beginning with the exam in 2018, you will have 55 minutes to answer the DBQ. It is recommended that you allot 15 minutes to prepare and the remaining 40 minutes to write your response.

All of the tips and strategies needed to answer a DBQ were gathered and presented in Units 8 & 9. Regularly review the **7 Steps for Writing a DBQ Essay** (page 144) and practice using the **DBQ Planner Worksheet** (page 172), and you will be prepared to achieve the highest score on this daunting section of the exam.

The Long Essay Question

The Long Essay Question (LEQ) makes up the last section of the AP U.S. History examination and counts for 15% of your total score on the exam. The LEQ requires you to develop a thesis or argument that is supported by specific, relevant evidence. You will be asked to select between three LEQ prompts and you will have 40 minutes (suggested time) to craft your answer. It is expected that you will use a specific Reasoning Skill as a means to explain and analyze a significant issue in United States history. If you have read through the lessons in this book and completed the exercises, you have acquired the necessary tools to answer this type of prompt successfully.

While the three questions in this section will be on different topics and from different time periods, they will ask you to examine the same Reasoning Skill (i.e., Continuity and Change over Time, Causation, or Comparison).

This book has emphasized that in order to score high on this essay, you must make certain you "describe as well as explain" the targeted Reasoning Skill as you develop your thesis or argument. Units 8 & 9 of this book have spelled out the steps you should take when planning and writing this important essay question.

How the Exam is Scored

The examination is graded in two phases. Immediately after the May testing, the multiple-choice answer sheets are machine graded by Educational Testing Service® (ETS) in New Jersey. The number of correct responses out of 49 questions is tallied, and that number is multiplied by a coefficient of 1.0612. Thus, a perfect score would be a 52 on the multiple-choice section, which accounts for 40 percent of the 130 total points a student can accumulate on the test. (See **Table 2** on page 202 for the complete scoring formula.)

The written portions of the exam are shipped to a grading site where nearly 1,200 high school and college history teachers gather to evaluate the answers. The graders are divided into tables of seven to eight readers, with a table leader assigned to each group to ensure productivity and accuracy during the grading. The table leader periodically rereads selected graded papers to ensure the readers are using the rubric properly and assigning fair and appropriate grades. Each grader is assigned an identification number to make sure that a reader grades only one portion of a student's exam.

Each short-answer question is divided into three parts, with each part worth a single point for a total of three points per question. The score of each short-answer is multiplied against a coefficient of 2.8887 and then added together for a total possible score of 26.

After becoming familiar with the scoring rubric for one of the two long essay question prompts or the DBQ, the readers begin grading. They will work on one of the three LEQ questions for the entire reading and score the papers on a six-point scale. Or, they may be assigned to the DBQ using a seven-point scale. Thus, a reader is likely to grade only one question during the reading— that is, one of the three LEQs or the DBQ. This eliminates the possibility that a student's entire essay grade will be determined by only one reader.

The LEQ and DBQ scores are both weighted so that they total 52 points when combined, the same value as the multiple-choice section. However, the DBQ is worth significantly more (67%) than the LEQ. As you saw in the rubrics, a student can earn as many as six points on the LEQ, which is multiplied by 3.25 for a total of 19.5 points. Likewise, a student can earn as many as seven points on the DBQ, which is multiplied by 4.6427 for a total of 32.5 points. (Again, see **Table 2** for the complete scoring formula.)

When all three written portions of the exam have been graded, the scores are combined with the multiple-choice score to yield a possible overall score of 130 points. All the student scores are then listed in a range from 0–130. From this list, the Chief Faculty Consultant (aka the Chief Reader) and ETS staff establish the specific number of points a student must accumulate in order to score a 5, 4, 3, 2, or 1 on the AP exam.

For example, in 2015 a student with a total score above 97 received a 5 on the test, and student with a score above 80 received a 4 (see **Table 1** below). These threshold levels will vary slightly from year to year, however, at the discretion of the team mentioned above. The final scores are then reported to students and their high schools or colleges in early July.

Table 1   AP U.S. History Score Conversion Chart

Composite Score Range	Final AP Score
0–43	1
44–62	2
63–79	3
80–96	4
97–130	5

Table 2 AP U.S. History Scoring Worksheet

Section I – Part A: Multiple-Choice Questions

$$\underline{\hspace{4cm}} \times \ 1.0612 \ = \ \underline{\hspace{4cm}}$$

<table>
<tr><td>Number Correct
(0–49)</td><td>Multiple-Choice Score
(0–52)</td></tr>
</table>

Section I – Part B: Short-Answer Questions

Question 1 $\underline{\hspace{3cm}} \times \ 2.8887 \ = \ \underline{\hspace{4cm}}$
            (0–3)

Question 2 $\underline{\hspace{3cm}} \times \ 2.8887 \ = \ \underline{\hspace{4cm}}$
            (0–3)

Question 3/4 $\underline{\hspace{3cm}} \times \ 2.8887 \ = \ \underline{\hspace{4cm}}$
            (0–3)

Total Short-Answer Score: $\underline{\hspace{3cm}}$
                                    (0–26)

Section II – Part A: Document-Based Question

$$\underline{\hspace{4cm}} \times \ 4.6427 \ = \ \underline{\hspace{4cm}}$$

<table>
<tr><td>(0–7)</td><td>DBQ Score (0–32.5)</td></tr>
</table>

Section II – Part B: Long Essay Question

$$\underline{\hspace{4cm}} \times \ 3.2500 \ = \ \underline{\hspace{4cm}}$$

<table>
<tr><td>(0–6)</td><td>LEQ Score (0–19.5)</td></tr>
</table>

Composite Score

Weighted Score 1:   Multiple-Choice Score   = $\underline{\hspace{4cm}}$

Weighted Score 2:   SAQ + DBQ + LEQ   = $\underline{\hspace{4cm}}$

$$\underline{\hspace{4cm}} \ + \ \underline{\hspace{4cm}} \ = \ \underline{\hspace{4cm}}$$

<table>
<tr><td>Weighted Section I
(0-52)</td><td>Weighted Section II
(0-78)</td><td>Total Composite Score
(0-130)</td></tr>
</table>

Answers & Explanations

Chapter 1: Separating Fact from Opinion

Exercise Prompt 1: *Why were the Inca and Aztec unable to defend their civilizations from conquest by the conquistadors?*

The first statement is a fact because most sources verify the Inca and Aztec were undermined when many of their captive subjects joined the conquistadors.

The second statement is an opinion. Who can prove that one culture is better than another? This statement reflects a bias.

The third statement is an opinion because it was not possible to measure the "smartness" of the Native Americans and the Spanish.

Exercise Prompt 2: *Why did the Europeans have an interest in Africa in the late 15ᵗʰ century?*

The first statement is an opinion. The idea of backwardness is a value judgment. It is not something that could be documented. It demonstrates a bias toward European development.

The second statement is an opinion. The psychology and sensitivity of Africans toward each other cannot be accurately measured or verified.

The third statement is a fact that many sources confirm. Africa and Europe had a robust trade in goods and slaves from the early 1500s until the end of the 18ᵗʰ century.

Chapter 2: Identifying the Purpose of the Question

Responses will vary.

Chapter 3: Determining Status Quo vs. Change

Part 1

Topic 1: The development of the African slave trade changed the exploration of the Western Hemisphere:

- allowed Europeans to exploit the hemisphere for gold/silver
- gave rise to cultivation of sugar in Caribbean
- allowed planters to shift from tobacco to sugar in Caribbean
- gave rise to the establishment of race-based servitude
- moved Europeans from a servant (indentured) system to chattel African slavery
- introduced diseases from Africa into the hemisphere
- gave rise to racial disparity with Africans greatly outnumbering whites throughout the Caribbean region
- promoted African cultural strands in hemisphere (music, foods, religious practices etc.)

Topic 2: The introduction of sugar/maize into people's diets promoted changes:

- as sugar demand grew so did the desire/need for slaves
- Caribbean shifted away from tobacco and other crops to sugar production
- made islands of Caribbean the most valuable colonies to European nations
- caused armed conflicts between European nations over sugar trade
- maize was discovered by Europeans and became a foundation of Columbian food exchange
- maize helped alleviate famine in Europe which enabled the surplus of people to colonize the Western Hemisphere
- maize became a staple crop of early European settlers

Part 2

Continuity	Change
- maintained animistic religious faith	- converted to Catholicism or Protestantism
- kept diet of maize, squash, beans etc.	- new foods introduced (rice, wheat, oats, etc.)
- maintained a form of village, town life	- new diseases introduced (small-pox, yellow fever, malaria, etc.)
- maintained many modes of trad-itional transportation (canoe etc.)	- enslaved
- maintained many aspects of family life (matrilineal)	- new types of animals introduced (horses, etc.)
- maintained many agricultural, hunting practices	- lost their gold and silver riches
	- formed alliances with Europeans
- maintained alliances with other tribes	- formed alliances with other Native Americans
- maintained concept of "collective sovereignty" of land ownership	- lost their cities, towns
	- lost their land

UNIT 2: The Colonial Period   1607–1754

Chapter 4: Creating Categories for Understanding

Promoted Religious Diversity	Represented Established Religion	Directly Challenged Religious Practices
Act of Toleration	Jonathan Edwards	Anne Hutchinson
Quakers	Anglican Church	Quakers
Roger Williams	Halfway Covenant	William Penn
First Great Awakening	Congregational Church	Roger Williams

Chapter 5: Using H.I.P.P.O. to Interpret Documents

Document 3

Historical Context: 1639, shortly after founding of colony and demonstrates the colonists' need to write down their rules of government.

Intended Audience: Residents of Windsor, Hartford, and Wethersfield (probably written by Thomas Hooker, founder of colony and John Hayes another prominent member of the colony)

Point of View: Good governments write down rules, government must be limited by general assembly meeting regularly and government will be religious-based, with only members of the church allowed to serve.

Purpose: To reinforce the need for written governmental rules to protect the people and to remind colonists that religion is important in maintaining peace and success in the colony.

Document 4

Historical Context: 1742, about seventy years after the colony was settled and is now thriving for white, indigo growing farmers and others involved in rice production.

Intended Audience: Her brother and possibly others who might be considering coming to South Carolina

Point of View: Life is good in South Carolina; opportunities are numerous for those who will work. It is the point of view of a "have" rather than a "have not."

Purpose: To encourage settlers to come to South Carolina and to justify the social and economic stratification that existed in the colony.

Chapter 6: What the Prompt is Asking You to Do

Time Period: 1607-1641

What to Do: Analyze the economic and social development of the two colonies. Include the founding of Virginia in 1607 and discuss Massachusetts through the final stages of the Great Migration in 1641. Note the prompt is about how people made a living (economics) and how they interacted with each other (social).

Content: Emphasize Virginia's dependence on tobacco and its reliance on slave labor. Contrast this with Massachusetts's diverse economy and its family-oriented social structure. You might also mention the religious contrast between the Anglican Church in Virginia and the Congregationalists (Puritans) in Massachusetts.

UNIT 3: The Revolution & the New Nation   1754–1800

Chapter 7: Linking Cause and Effect

Townshend Acts Effects:

- Showed British weakness
- Colonial protests
- Colonial violence
- Strengthened committees of correspondence
- Repeal of act strengthened radicals
- Colonial economic boycott

Coercive Acts Effects:

- Unified the colonies
- Designed to punish Massachusetts for the Boston Tea Party

- Demonstrated the oppression of the British government
- Prompted the calling of the First Continental Congress

Sugar Act Effects:

- First attempt to tax colonies after French and Indian War
- Angered colonies

Boston Massacre Effects:

- Death of five colonists
- Gave fuel to revolutionary fires
- Created martyrs to the cause

Stamp Act Effects:

- Colonial protests
- Colonial violence
- Creation of the Sons of Liberty
- Established colonial revolutionary rhetoric
- Colonial economic boycott
- Repeal strengthened radicals
- Unified the colonists

Salutary Neglect Effects:

- Allowed colonies to prosper economically
- Gave a feeling of independence to colonies

Stamp Act Congress Effects:

- Promoted colonial unity
- Reinforced idea that rights were endangered
- Called for colonial boycott
- Petitioned the king for help

Boston Tea Party Effects:

- Enraged the British
- Gave rise to the Coercive Acts
- Gave fuel to revolutionary fires

Chapter 8: Establishing the Credibility of Documents

Set 1: Who Fired First?

Document 2

P. It is a secondary source.

0. It was written in 1832, many years after the event.

W. The author is a British officer and possessed a biased view.

S. He was at the scene, but the years may have dulled his memory.

The better source is Document 1. In Set 1, the Fessenden document has more credibility because it is an eyewitness account written only four days after the battle. In addition, as an observer, he had a vantage point to see what went on. He also offered the testimony under oath. Granted, he may not have been completely objective because he may have favored the colonial side, but the second source has even more problems. It was written many years after the fact, and the author was a British soldier, so he would definitely have had a partisan view.

Set 2: What Caused the Revolution?

Document 3

P. It is a secondary source.

O. It was written in 1954, many years after the fact.

W. The author is an American historian. While he is dedicated to discovering the truth in the past, he might be more favorable to the American point of view.

S. The writer is not an eyewitness to, or participant in, the event.

Document 4

P. It is a primary source.

O. It was written at the time of the upheaval and rebellion.

W. He was a partisan, but he had a good view of why the rebellion developed.

S. He was a participant in the events and helped steer the rebellion.

The better source is Document 4. In Set 2, the source by John Dickinson has more credibility. It was written by one of the participants of the Revolution and was drafted at the height of the imperial crisis. The first document is a secondary source written in the 1950s. While it offers a nice summary and perspective, we must give more credence to a primary source written at the time of the event.

Chapter 9: Making Inferences to Expand Meaning

Document 2 – Inferences:

a. The Alien and Sedition Acts are just and necessary.

b. Foreigners were not welcome in America in the 1790s.

c. America needed to protect itself from foreigners.

d. If you were loyal, you would not be affected by the acts.

e. Only the dishonest and lawless challenged the acts.

f. Freedom is not unlimited.

g. Unstrained freedom could endanger the country.

Chapter 10: Contextualizing Events

Relationship *during* Salutary Neglect Era	Relationship *after* Salutary Neglect Ended
- Parliament had supreme authority in empire	- French and Indian War altered relationship
- Navigation Acts applied to all in the empire	- Colonists objected to Parliament's taxes
- Army protected the colonies from Indians	- France removed as a colonial threat
- Army protected the colonies from the French	- Army now seen as oppressor not protector
- Englishmen abroad were protected by British Constitution	- Rights of colonials not being protected
- Colonial militia were a source of manpower	- Colonial assemblies should levy taxes
- Britain left colonies alone to govern themselves	- Britain restricted colonial westward expansion
- English merchants profited from colonies	- British requisition and recruitment policies were oppressive and unfair in colonies
- Taxes in colony were often ignored and not paid	
- Navigation Acts often ignored without consequences	- British officials were contemptible of colonial militia's fighting abilities
	- Britain tried to reorganize the North American colonies
	- British taxing policy seemed unfair

Chapter 11: Analyzing Secondary Sources

Francis Parkman was more positive about the outcome of the French and Indian War on Britain's place in the world than Anderson and Cayton. He believed the war made England the only real world power at the time and that—in the short run at least—the conflict was a glorious event.

UNIT 4: Jeffersonian Era & Age of Jackson   1800–1848

Chapter 12: Using Graphs and Maps Effectively

Louisiana Purchase Map

1. The United States gained control of the Mississippi River, eliminated the French from its border, and provided several generations with rich farmland.

2. The South, because slavery would have room to spread, and the West, because as the nation expanded this region would have greater political and economic power.

3. Native Americans and New Englanders saw their role in politics and society further diluted, as did the Spanish, who now had Americans for neighbors.

4. By gaining control of the Mississippi, doubling the size of the nation, and eliminating the French threat, the U.S. was a stronger, more secure nation.

American Exports Graph

1. American exports went through boom and bust periods.

2. The U.S. placed various levels of embargo on its own exports from 1807 to 1812. This is reflected in the great drop after 1807. As we modified the embargoes in 1808–1810, exports recovered somewhat.

When France and England were at war from 1793 to 1803, exports boomed. During a temporary peace, exports dropped, but expanded again when armed conflict resumed in 1805. The war with England, 1812–1814, practically eliminated exports.

3. American exports were dependent on both domestic and foreign forces from 1790 to 1815.

Chapter 13: Establishing Point of View

Did Jackson and Calhoun support or oppose the following?

Issue	Jackson's Point of View	Calhoun's Point of View	Discussion
Tariff of Abominations	Mildly Opposed	Strongly Opposed	Jackson opposed high tariffs in general, yet they were necessary until the national debt was paid. Calhoun believed tariffs hurt the South, and feared the growing power of the central government.
The Market Revolution	Opposed	Opposed	Both men, as southern slaveholders, opposed the growing industrial, mercantile power of the North.
Nullification of laws	Very strongly opposed	Supported	Jackson saw nullification as a threat to the Union. Calhoun believed the states must be protected from the national government.
Indian Removal Act	Supported	Supported	Both agreed: Indians were in the way of southern cotton expansion.

Issue	Jackson's Point of View	Calhoun's Point of View	Discussion
Exposition and Protest	Very strongly opposed	Supported	Jackson saw ideas as a step to disunion. Calhoun wrote it and believed the South must be protected.
Use of the Spoils System	Supported	Supported	Both men wanted new people in the government—especially southerners.

Chapter 14: Using Documents in an Essay

Responses will vary.

Chapter 15: Using Contrasting Documents

Responses will vary, but a theme that could be developed in your paragraph is how Calhoun's views moved from a strong nationalist during his time as Secretary of War, to a sectionalist during his role as spokesman for southern rights in the late 1820s and beyond. You might also connect his sectional views to those of another time period by linking them to people like Edmund Ruffin and Jefferson Davis in the 1850s and 1860s (synthesis).

Chapter 16: Developing a Thesis

Statement 3 is the strongest thesis to use to answer the question posed in **Exercise Prompt 1**. It passes the A. C. I. D. test.

   ✓   **A**ll aspects of topic dealt with

✓ <u>C</u>lear position is taken on the issues

✓ <u>I</u>nfrastructure in place to build essay upon

✓ <u>D</u>irectly addresses the topic

While statement 1 takes a position on the issue and directly addresses the topic, it is too narrow as it deals with only one aspect of the disagreements among the abolitionists and does not supply an infrastructure. Statement 2 is too general and vague.

Answers will vary in response to **Exercise Prompt 2.** A possible thesis statement might included: "While the abolitionist movement supplied both strategies and personnel for the early women's movement, it also drained away attention and resources from women's issues in the 1840s."

Chapter 17: Contextualization and Chart Analysis

The Five T's

Time: 1810-1860

Topics: Women's Population, Age, and Child Bearing

Trends: The overall number of women was growing rapidly; they were having fewer babies and they were living longer.

Tie Trends to Cause:

- women's health care improved;

- the women's movement gained some tractions so women had more control over reproduction;

- the slight increase from 1850-1860 may reflect more young immigrants coming into the nation and having more babies

The implication: Women's quality of life improved: better health, living longer, fewer child-rearing responsibilities, growing component of U.S. population. A context for the women's movement of the 1840s and 1850s as they worked to gain a better life from women.

UNIT 5: Manifest Destiny to Reconstruction   1844–1877

Chapter 18: Extending and Modifying a Thesis

Exercise Prompt 1

Clarifying Question: How did southern actions and demands convince the North that a slave power conspiracy existed?

Positive Thesis: The South, through its attempt to extend slavery and to repeal the Missouri Compromise, supported Northern contentions that a slave power was conspiring against them and their way of life.

Exercise Prompt 2

Clarifying Question: Would stronger American action have resulted in British concessions in Oregon?

Negative Thesis: Rather than cowardly, President Polk's Oregon policy was prudent and based on a realistic assessment of America's national interest in 1846.

Exercise Prompt 3

Clarifying Question: Did the land acquired in 1848 help or hurt American development?

Positive/Negative Thesis: While the land acquired in 1848 caused sectional turmoil and conflict, it also provided valuable economic and national security benefits for the United States for many years to come.

Chapter 19: Cartoons and Contextualization

Date: 1844 and its context

Action: Clay and Polk are trying to climb the nomination pole to become their party's standard bearer in 1844. Polk, as the dark horse, seems to have a steeper climb.

Important People/Objects: Henry Clay, James K. Polk, Thomas Hart Benton, Andrew Jackson, John C. Calhoun

Label: Political Climbing Boys – the illustrator is making a point that the Whigs (Clay) had an easier climb to the nomination than the Democrats with Polk, who seemed to need convincing by his supporters to seek the nomination.

Y (Why): It was created to show the ups and downs of the nominating process in 1844. Also, the drawing may have represented the illustrator's view that the Whigs were in a better position than the Democrats, at least at the outset, to win the White House in the upcoming election.

Chapter 20: Comparing and Contrasting Historical Positions

Andrew Johnson vs. the Radical Republicans
Similarities and Differences

President Johnson

Radicals

Believed president in charge of Reconstruction

States should handle radical issues

Blacks should not vote

No federal help for Freedmen

Opposed Freedmen's Bureau

Opposed the 14th Amendment

Used veto 20 times

South must be punished

Treason must be made odious

Lincoln's death must be avenged

Slavery must be ended

Planter class must be punished

Violence in South must stop

Believed Congress in charge

Federal gov't should regulate race relations

Some whites should not vote

Freedmen should receive gov't aid

Federal gov't role in society should grow

Supported the 14th Amendment

Overrode veto 19 times

Chapter 21: Using Documents and Charts in an Essay

From **Document 3**, you might find:

- The South was dependent on the North for manufactured goods;
- The South was agrarian and rural;
- The South lacked artistic achievements;
- The North was outdistancing the South in population;
- Immigrants would not settle in the South;
- Southern population was not very diverse;
- The North controlled the money the South needed.

From **Document 4**, you might find:

- The Northeastern states in 1860 had 10 times the manufacturing population of the South;
- The Northeastern manufacturing population grew 27% from 1850 to 1860;
- The South's manufacturing population grew 15% from 1850 to 1860;
- The North Central manufacturing population grew faster than both the North and the South;
- The South had only about 1 in 12 people living in a city in 1860;
- The North had about 1 in 3 people living in a city;
- By 1860, the South was far less industrialized or urbanized than the northern states.

Paragraphs will vary.

UNIT 6: America Transformed   1865–1898

Chapter 22: Recognizing Relevant Evidence

Statement 1 is irrelevant. The farmers did not call for food regulation. That came later under the progressive reformers in the early 1900s.

Statement 2 is relevant. The Omaha Platform did call for government ownership and regulation of railroads, which became a mainstay of American reform in the late 19th century.

Statement 3 is irrelevant. The Populists did not ask for the government payment to farmers. That was a New Deal farm policy in the 1930s.

Statement 4 is relevant. A major goal of the Populists was expansion of the money supply by "free silver." These pressures made gold vs. silver a major issue in the 1896 election.

Chapter 23: Using Facts to Support a Thesis

Exercise Prompt 1: *Evaluate the extent to which the industrialists of the last quarter of the 19th century were visionaries, rather than "robber barons."*

The best choice is Statement 3. It has specific information about how the industrialists made America competitive with other countries, but it also suggests how they abused Americans at home. Statement 1 is too general and vague to develop the thesis. Statement 2 is an opinion about the industrialists and is not backed up with facts or proof.

Exercise Prompt 2: *Evaluate the extent to which the Populists' program of the 1890s offered acceptable solutions to the problems in American society.*

The best choice is Statement 2. It makes reference to several planks of the Omaha platform and supports the thesis in a concrete manner. Statement 1 is too general and does not really defend the thesis with concrete information. Statement 3 is an opinion.

Chapter 24: Using Documents and Cartoons in an Essay

In analyzing **Document 3**, you should see:

- Bryan is sowing discord between the classes;
- He sees division between cities and rural areas;
- Lots of us vs. them;
- Gold vs. silver;
- Talks of fights, struggle, confrontations;
- Sees rural people as persecuted by cities and the gold standard;
- Sees rural areas as superior to the cities;
- Fighting the rising tide of urbanization;
- Bryan is challenging the status quo.

In analyzing the cartoon in **Document 4**, you should see that:

- McKinley was a Civil War veteran;
- Outside information: Republicans still waving the bloody shirt;
- McKinley was a grownup, mature;
- Bryan was immature;
- Outside information: Bryan only 36 at time of election;
- Bryan had little experience;
- Bryan is playing a rattle (noisy), a dig at his inflammatory speeches.

In analyzing **Document 5**, you should see:

- Harlan is calling for the Constitution to be color blind;
- No citizen regardless of race should be denied their rights;
- Laws that are race based represent servitude and degradation;
- All Americans should be equal before the bar of justice;
- Harlan opposed separate railroad cars for Blacks and Whites;
- Harlan believed the *Plessy v. Ferguson* was wrong both legally and morally;
- In *Plessy* the doctrine of separate but equal was put into place and remained so until 1954;

- Harlan was the lone dissenter in the case that was decided 7-1;
- Harlan had made dissents early in civil rights cases in the 1880s;
- The *Plessy* decision gave the federal government's imprimatur (approval) to the Jim Crow system.

In analyzing the cartoon in **Document 6,** you should see:

- The peaceful voting of Freedmen after the war;
- The fruits of the Civil War for African Americans;
- The man first in line is a worker or field hand—demonstrating the changes brought on by the Civil War;
- 1867 was a high time for Radical Republicans in Congress;
- Black soldiers were offered the right to vote for their service;
- Some Blacks (man 2nd in line) were professionals and prosperous;
- The observer of the voting process looked on with benign approval;
- The federal government protected Black rights briefly after the war;
- The 15th Amendment put voting rights for the men in the cartoon into the Constitution;
- The vote was lost by poll taxes, literacy tests, and grandfather clauses;

Theses and paragraphs will vary.

UNIT 7: America and the World   1890–1945

Chapter 25: Bias and Point of View

1. Emilio Aguinaldo

Answer: He would say that the New Manifest Destiny was flawed.

Bias: As the leader of the Filipino rebellion and a strong nationalist, he saw the contradictions in American claims of spreading liberty and democracy while denying those privileges to colonial peoples.

2.   Josiah Strong

Answer: He would not see flaws in the New Manifest Destiny.

Bias: He was an intellectual defender of the expansion policy, and his academic and religious standing would be damaged by any criticism of the policy.

3.   George Dewey

Answer: He would not see a flaw in the New Manifest Destiny or in the crushing of the insurrection.

Bias: As a naval officer, Dewey was the "sword of expansion in the 1890s." He followed his orders, but he also benefited as expansion enhanced his reputation and the importance of the military in American life.

Chapter 26: Interpreting Secondary Sources

a)   Kolko and Chambers viewed the impact of the Progressive Era through differing historical lenses. Chambers believed that movement modernized America and established a positive social agenda. On the other hand, Kolko saw the progressives as essentially conservative people who preserved the capitalist system with all its economic, political, and social shortcomings.

b)   The distribution of income remained unchanged during these reform years; the rich remain rich and the poor failed to improve their lot; ownership of the means of production remained the same with the same powerful people in charge as before the turn of the century; the three Progressive Presidents (Theodore Roosevelt, William H. Taft, and Woodrow Wilson) were all recognized as conservatives and defenders of the status quo.

c)   The progressives began the process of government regulation of the abuses of big business that would continue throughout the 20th century; social services such as drug/food regulations were established; children were protected in the work place; settlement houses began to lay the foundation for a national safety net.

Chapter 27: Grouping Documents into Categories

Pro (+)	Con (–)
Document 2	Document 1
Document 4	Document 3

Sample Rationale: The prompt and thesis statement would be supported by documents that indicate Wilson played a significant role in defeating the treaty in 1919–1920. These sources would highlight his refusal to compromise with his opponents. Document 2 and Document 4 are examples of these sources. In Document 2, Wilson tells his supporters to vote against the treaty when it included the Lodge reservations. In Document 4, he suggests that the American people must choose between the League of Nations as he wants it, or withdraw from contact with the allies (no room for compromise).

Documents 1 and 3 suggest that Wilson was not completely at fault in the rejection of the League. Document 1 shows how deep isolationist feelings flowed in America after the war. Document 3 highlights Senator Lodge's role in using the reservationists to the treaty to block its ratification.

Chapter 28: Creating an Introductory Paragraph

Sample introductory paragraph on Booker T. Washington's policies:
At first Booker T. Washington was realistic in his approach to fighting Jim Crow, but his philosophy failed to change with the times. Washington's advice to accept social and political segregation in return for economic opportunities did make slight changes for African Americans, but by the early 1900s, he was outdated. In the short run, by suggesting that blacks accept the discrimination of the Jim Crow system, his ideas represented both continuity and change. He raised money for Tuskegee and provided support for a few African American initiatives, but overall little really changed

in the lives of African Americans from 1895–1915. A review of Washington's views and the challenges he faced will demonstrate that more remained the same than changed for Black Americans in this era.

Chapter 29: Writing a Concluding Paragraph

Answers will vary. A concluding paragraph could contain some of the following ideas in its summary:

Exercise Prompt 1:

- Events of the 1930s favored the isolationists, but when Hitler conquered Europe the internationalists became more influential;

- Because of economic troubles, the country wanted to stay out of European affairs;

- The Neutrality Acts demonstrated the power of the isolationists

- As the Nazis conquered Europe, Americans became anxious, repealed the Neutrality Acts, and began Lend Lease;

- The struggle between the isolationists and internationalists was part of an on-going struggle that had its roots in the battle over the League of Nations after the Great War (synthesis);

- And this struggle would continue as America entered the Cold War as a world power (synthesis).

Exercise Prompt 2:

- The U.S. suffered significant losses at Iwo Jima and Okinawa

- The planned invasion of Japan scheduled for November might cost 1 million American causalities

- The U.S. considered the impact of the bombs on the Russians, but that was secondary to the military situation in 1945

- While the U.S. and U.S.S.R. were allies, the Soviets were not living up to their pledges related to the Atlantic Charter

- The Atomic bombs were not useful diplomatic weapons

- The Russians were not intimidated by the bombs and had spies at Los Alamos monitoring the progress of the weapon's development

- As a new President, Truman needed to use every weapon at his disposal to end the war

- The Japanese were fighting to the death to protect their Emperor and way of life

Concluding paragraphs will vary.

UNIT 8: The Cold War & the American Dream   1945–1980

Chapter 30: Prioritizing Facts in Planning an Essay

Exercise Prompt 1: *How successful was President Dwight D. Eisenhower in containing communism in Europe between 1953 and 1961?*

  4   The Geneva Conference of 1954

  1   Peaceful coexistence with the USSR

  3   The Hungarian uprising in 1956

  2   Strengthening NATO

Rationale: Peaceful coexistence was most successful because it maintained peace and allowed Eisenhower to keep the country safe while he reduced defense spending. The second most useful fact is the strengthening of NATO, which kept the peace in Europe and contained communism. The Hungarian revolution was not a success at all. It tarnished Eisenhower's pledge to roll back communism. The least effective fact is the Geneva Conference of 1954, which was about Asia, not European issues.

Exercise Prompt 2: *Which of the following events was the most serious blow to America's international prestige in the Cold War?*

  4   The Cuban Missile Crisis

  3   The Camp David Accords

___1___ The Bay of Pigs Invasion

___2___ The Iran-Contra Affair

Rationale: The Bay of Pigs made the U.S. look like an inept, imperialistic power. Although primarily a domestic problem, the Iran-Contra Affair hurt America by showing that the executive branch did not follow the law. The Camp David Accords did not hurt American prestige; they actually expanded its role in the Middle East. The least useful fact would be the Cuban Missile Crisis because America handled it peacefully and well, and our prestige was enhanced.

Chapter 31: Sequencing Evidence in an Essay

Point of view: Lyndon Johnson did more for African Americans than any other U.S. president.

___2___ In 1964, President Johnson got a landmark civil rights bill through Congress.

___5___ President Kennedy did more for African Americans than Lyndon Johnson.

___1___ President Johnson, as a southern conservative, surprised many African Americans with his strong advocacy of civil rights in the mid-1960s.

___4___ The racial unrest of 1966–1967 tarnished President Johnson's accomplishments in civil rights.

___3___ President Johnson appointed Thurgood Marshall, the first African American Supreme Court justice.

Rationale: The statement about Johnson as a surprising supporter of civil rights would serve nicely as a topic sentence for a paragraph in the argument. The passage of the Civil Rights Act of 1964 is good support for the first statement. Johnson's appointment of Marshall to the Supreme Court is useful in proving the argument, but not as meaningful as the Civil Right Act. The racial unrest hurt Johnson's reputation and probably belongs in a concession paragraph later in the paper. The Kennedy comparison is an opinion and should not be included in the argument.

Chapter 32: Steps for Writing a DBQ Essay

Below are several possible responses to the areas of the planner that were left blank. Sample responses to this prompt can be found on the companion website. Go to **www.sherpalearning.com/skillbook**.

Step 1 – Task Discuss suggested response provided on page 150.

> **Time Period** 1945-1964 (The post war era is a rich topic for contextualizing the causes of the Civil Rights movement in the 1950s and 1960s.)

Step 2 – Clarifying Question What caused the Civil Rights movement to take off in the 1950s and what resistance was there to it?

Step 3 – Thesis Answers will vary.

Step 4 – Possible Outside Information

- John Kennedy
- Jackie Robinson
- Eugene "Bull" Connor
- "To Secure These Rights"
- Dixiecrats (States Right Party)
- Great Migration
- New Frontier
- Civil Rights Act 1963
- Southern Christian Leadership
- Conference
- Bayard Rustin
- Roy Wilkins
- Executive Order 9981
- Birmingham Church Bombing
- Civil Rights Act of 1957/1960
- March on Washington 1963
- Strom Thurmond
- Sit-In Demonstrations
- Great Society
- Montgomery Bus Boycott
- James Meredith
- A. Philip Randolph
- *Seatt v. Painter*
- N.A.C.C.P.

Step 5 – Document Analysis (H.I.P.P.O.) Answers will vary.

Step 6 – Pro and Con Categories

Pro	Con
Document 1 (Brown Decision started racial revolution)	Document 3 (Southern resistance to Brown)
Document 2 (Bus boycott made King a national leader)	Document 4 (Little Rock's resistance to school integration)
Document 5 (Freedom Riders attempt to desegregate interstate bus travel)	Document 5 (Violent resistance to changes)
Document 6 (King's Letter from jail expresses philosophy behind his movement)	Document 7 (Shows some resistance to Civil Rights Act of 1964)
Document 7 (A majority of Americans support Civil Rights Act)	*Note: some documents can be used as both pro and con*

Step 7 – Background (Contextualization) Discussions regarding the suggested response on page 151 will vary.

Chapter 33: Steps for Writing an LEQ Essay

While your answers to the various sections of the LEQ Planner Worksheet will vary, below are several possible responses to the areas of the planner that were left blank. Sample responses to this prompt can be found on the companion website. Go to **www.sherpalearning.com/skillbook**.

Step 1 – Reasoning Skill Causation (cause and effect)

  Content Area Cold War developments in both Europe and Asia from 1943–1961.

Step 3 – Facts You Know (partial list provided; below are some other possible facts, though answers will vary)

- Harry Truman
- Potsdam Conference
- Teheran Conference
- Nikita Khrushchev
- John Foster Dulles
- Berlin Air Lift
- Iron Curtain
- Winston Churchill
- Hungarian Revolt
- East German Revolt
- U-2 flights
- Korean War
- Douglas MacArthur
- 1st Indochina War
- Ngo Dinh Diem

- Ho Chi Minh
- Geneva Conference
- Atlantic Charter
- Brinkmanship
- Truman Doctrine
- Eisenhower Doctrine
- Dien Bien Phu
- atomic bombs
- Mohammed Mossadegh
- appeasement
- Jacob Arbenz
- Dwight Eisenhower
- Dean Acheson
- Joe Stalin

Step 5 – Categories of Facts   Partial list provided

Step 8 – Supporting Paragraphs   Answers will vary

Step 9 – Concluding Paragraph   Answers will vary

UNIT 9: America Redefined   1981–Present

Chapter 34: A Review of the Disciplinary Practices and Reasoning Skills

1. By contextualizing historical developments, you connect events of one time period to related events and phenomena in another era. To some degree, this is why we study history. It offers background on the present and provides perspective on current problems and who we are and have been. Contextualization helps students relate the

past to the present and to gain a more meaningful understanding of history and themselves. In short, the process is a tool that enriches both personal and national identity.

2.   Answers will vary.

3.   The ability to analyze historical documents is the life blood in the study of history. It is this process that allows a student to formulate hypotheses about the past, and to create the resources necessary to support their thesis as they develop written arguments. In addition, document analysis gives students a direct avenue to the voices of the past without the filter of a teacher or textbook.

4.   The danger of connecting causes too quickly to events is that it may preclude or even stop a deeper investigation of a topic or problem. You may be making a rush to judgment. Rarely is an event caused simply by one factor. The complexity of human activities is almost always attributable to multiple causes. By reducing a problem to one quick, simple cause, you are likely to make an inadequate or partial analysis of the topic under consideration, and undercut the strength of your argument.

5.   Comparison and contextualization are similar types of skills in that both ask you to link facts together and, in some cases, suggest how these connections are related to larger issues. As you make an argument by comparing and/or contrasting particular circumstances, you often employ developments in one era with events in another time or place (contextualization). You may be called upon to explain how a different setting is similar-yet-different from the period targeted in the prompt.

6.   Answers will vary.

Chapter 35: Writing a DBQ Essay

Exercise Question: *Evaluate the extent to which the conflict over Vietnam changed American political and social beliefs in the 1960s.*

Themes

Overall, thesis should address the skill of causation and the effects of the war on America's social and political structure.

Putting the war into a context of changes from the 1950s and early 1960s:

- Many saw the Eisenhower years as a conservative, staid time in America
- Most Americans trusted the government to tell the truth
- The Cold War tensions were very high
- America's place and power in the world seemed secure
- Blacks were still sorting out the implications of the Brown decision and a means for achieving equal rights
- Women accepted a traditional role in the house and society
- College students accepted the rules of their school—did not challenge the curriculum or the place of the university in American society
- College students played a minor role in politics

Changes brought on by the Vietnam War:

- The war called into question the domino theory and America's ability to transform other countries in its own image
- Vietnam shook America's faith in itself and its political leaders
- Vietnam made Americans question the truthfulness of their government
- Vietnam got young people involved in changing political policies
- Vietnam and civil rights transformed many young people into activists who did not accept the values of their parents, corporations, or the government
- Vietnam derailed the Civil Rights Movement as spending priorities changed and young, poor blacks were sent to fight
- The war raised the issue of "guns vs. butter"
- Many young people lost faith in the government and society in the 1960s

- Protest spawned an alternative lifestyle among many involving drugs and casual sex

- Protests went beyond politics to include career choice, dress, and hairstyle

- A nascent women's movement gained momentum

Document Use

Document 1: Johnson still talked of America keeping its word and domino theory, believed victory was very possible in Vietnam. Connect with Document 2. Continuation of traditional Cold War ideas. Document represents the point of view of President Johnson that we must not cut and run in Vietnam. It was the grounds for his escalation of the war in 1965–1968.

Document 2: Expresses main belief about Vietnam in 1961: vital to American security, democracy vs. communism, domino theory in play, use military option to gain American goals. Document represents the prevailing point of view of government officials at the beginning of the 1960s.

Document 3: Young people saw their differences with past generations. They believed they could transform society; rejected racial bias, war. Idealism that drove the Civil Rights Movement and antiwar movement. Clearly questioned past role for young. Document represents the point of view of the growing radicalism of the youth movement in the early 1960s.

Document 4: Congress also saw flaws in America's Vietnam policy. Tried to do too much. Leaders were not aware of limits and could not match means with ends. Questioned America's post-World War II ability to transform world. Document represents the point of view of people who questioned whether the U.S. was on the right track in Vietnam. It was the foundation of the growing anti-war movement in the mid and late 1960s.

Document 5: Vietnam divided old allies. King believed the war took valuable resources from War on Poverty and civil rights battle. Also raised the racial and class issue about the draft. War began to split the Great Society coalition. Document represents the point of view of civil rights leaders over the deleterious effect the war was having on minorities and the civil rights movement as the conflict crowded out resources and focus for improving African-American's place in society.

Document 6: Statistics can be used several ways: proof that King was right about how resources were being drained from domestic issues to fight war. (From 1965 to 1968, defense spending increased by $31 million; health by only $11.2 million; and education by $5.0 million.) On the other hand, in the same period, spending for these areas was up over fourfold. This document could be used in a concession paragraph to demonstrate that Johnson tried to keep his commitments in Vietnam and also to the war, which caused inflation later on. The chart represents the point of view of both those who said we could have guns and butter in the 1960s and those that claimed valuable resources were being wasted on a faraway war.

Document 7: Demonstrates the impact of war, protest on the most radical nonpolitical members of the counterculture. Cynical view of America dedicated to dropping out and using drugs. Contrast it with Document 2 and the idealism of the early 1960s. Document represents the point of view of the counter culture, and/or the "hippies" who were alienated by the war and its impact on America in the 1960s.

Possible Outside Information

- Domino Theory
- Student Non-Violent Coordinating Committee
- Gulf of Tonkin Resolution
- Free Speech Movement
- Viet Cong Ngo
- Dinh Diem
- War on Poverty
- Rolling Thunder
- Eugene McCarthy
- March on Pentagon
- Counterculture
- Civil Rights Acts
- Containment
- Martin Luther King
- Tet Offensive
- Appeasement
- Baby boom
- Ho Chi Minh
- Woodstock
- Great Society
- Robert Kennedy
- Hippies
- Bob Dylan
- New Left
- Students for a Democratic Society
- Betty Freidan

- The Feminine Mystique
- Sit-ins
- Freedom Rides
- Civil Rights Acts, 1964, 1965

- Black Power
- Richard Nixon
- Chicago riots, 1968

Chapter 36: Writing an LEQ Essay

Exercise Prompt 1: *Evaluate the extent to which the American Revolution contributed to maintaining continuity as well as fostered change in America's political, social, and economic relations from 1776–1789.*

Themes

Themes of Continuity:

- The planters, lawyers, and merchants remained at the top of society
- Slavery remained in place in the southern colonies
- Individual states maintained their sovereignty
- Overall major trading patterns with Europe maintained
- Violent protest to government policies continued
- Women's inferior place in society maintained
- Native American conflicts over land continued
- Republicanism defined as an exclusively white enterprise
- Property requirement remained for voting in most states
- Continued conflict with Great Britain over trade and finances
- Continued conflict with Spain over use of the Mississippi River
- Bills of Rights highlighted in state constitutions and charters

Themes of Change:

- Thousands of Loyalists left, opening up social/economic opportunities
- Many northern states put slavery on road to extinction
- The Constitution reigned in the excesses of liberty from Revolution
- Republican ideals of government emerged
- Educational opportunities for women expanded
- Governments sought direct authorization from the people
- Checks and balances introduced to limit power of government
- Attempts made to contain the expansion of slavery
- Less power for executives and more power for legislatures
- Manumission of slaves increased
- Greater freedom of religion—separation of church and state
- Reduced role of government in economy
- Indentured servant system weakened
- Previous patterns of social deference were weakened and destroyed

Possible Outside Information

- Articles of Confederation
- Constitution
- Shays's Rebellion
- Fries's Rebellion
- Society of Cincinnati
- Charles Montesquieu
- Anglican Church
- Virginia Plan
- James Madison
- Alexander Hamilton
- George Washington
- Thomas Jefferson
- Northwest Ordinance
- Adam Smith
- Coverture
- Republican Motherhood
- Treaty of Fort Stanwix (1785)
- Treaty of Paris (1783)
- Loyalists (Tories)

Exercise Prompt 2: *Evaluate the extent to which the demand for currency reform contributed to maintaining continuity as well as fostered change in America from 1870–1900.*

Themes

Themes of Continuity:

- Gold standard remained the main source of currency
- Gov't reinforced the gold standard during Depression of 1893
- Churches endorsed the virtue of hard money over paper currency
- Withdrawal of greenback dollars after Civil War
- Farm prices remained low and declined 1870-1900
- Railroad and bankers remained villainous controllers of economy
- Farmers' debt continued to grow
- Congress removed silver as a currency in 1873
- Election of 1896 reflected nation's faith in gold standard
- Millions of Americans still saw farm ownership as the American Dream

Themes of Change:

- Calls for return of silver as a currency
- Call for the reissuance of greenback paper currency
- Rise of the Populist Party and "free silver" movement
- Government began to use silver as well as gold as currency standard
- Rise of the Grange and Greenback Labor Party
- Farmers shifted to commercial farming—one cash crop
- Farmers became small-time business men—concerned with interest rates and railroad policies
- Calls for more government regulation and control of economy
- Farmers attempted to organize themselves into political parties
- Attacks directed at "money power" in the eastern United States
- Mechanization boosted productivity, but drove down prices

Possible Outside Information

- Mint Act of 1792
- Legal Tender Act 1870
- Resumption Act 1875
- Bland Allison Act 1878
- Sherman Silver Act 1890
- William "Coins" Harvey
- The Populist Party
- Greenback Labor Party
- Peter Cooper
- James B. Weaver
- The Crime of '73

- Oliver H. Kelley
- Charles Macune
- Mary E. Lease
- Thomas Watson
- "free silver"
- William Jennings Bryan
- William McKinley
- Farmers' Alliances
- Jerry Simpson
- Omaha Platform
- Panic of 1893

Exercise Prompt 3: *Evaluate the extent to which the presidency of Ronald Reagan contributed to maintaining continuity as well as fostered change in America during the 1980s and beyond.*

Themes

Themes of Continuity:

- Overall New Deal welfare state remained intact
- Maintained Social Security and Medicare
- Kept Civil Rights Acts of 1964, 1965
- Continuity to negotiate with U.S.S.R.
- Signed arms reduction treaties as predecessors had done
- Continued the containment of communism
- Maintained the Department of Education (size of government)
- Did not push extreme conservative social agenda (school prayer, ban on abortion)

Themes of Change:

- Pledged to roll back size of government
- Pledged to roll back many Great Society programs
- Confronted the Soviet Union as an "evil empire"
- Cut taxes (in short run)
- Named first woman to the Supreme Court
- Brought inflation under control after two decades
- Put New Deal liberalism on the defensive
- Believed: "The government is not the solution to our problems, government is the problem"
- Accelerated the conservative movement that had been growing for over twenty years
- Began the end of the Cold War

Possible Outside Information

- Jimmy Carter
- John Anderson
- Assassination attempt March 1981
- Reaganomics
- Economic Recovery Tax Act
- David Stockman
- Sandra Day O'Connor
- Evil Empire

- Strategic Defense Initiative (Star Wars)
- Contras
- Walter Mondale
- Geraldine Ferraro
- George H. W. Bush
- Iran-Contra Affair
- Oliver North
- Mikhail Gorbachev

Chapter 37: Understanding the DBQ and LEQ Rubrics

Discussions of the two rubrics will vary.

Acknowledgments

Sherpa Learning, LLC. has made every effort to obtain permission for the reprinting of all selections contained herein. If any author is not acknowledged, please contact the publisher for proper acknowledgment in all future editions or reprintings of this book.

Photographs & Illustrations:

p. 1, Library of Congress; p. 13, North Wind Picture Archives; p. 25, lithograph by Clay, Cosack, & Co., based on the painting by Archibald Willard, Library of Congress; p. 45, lithograph by A.A. Hoffay, Library of Congress; p. 73, New York Public Library; p. 81, woodcut and letterpress with watercolor, published by Huestis & Co. and Robert Elton, Library of Congress; p. 83, New York Public Library; p. 93, photo by Lewis Wickes Hine, Library of Congress; p. 104, cartoon by Thomas Nast from Harper's Weekly, August 9, 1884; p. 107, cartoon by W.A. Rogers from Harper's Weekly, August 29, 1896; p. 107, cartoon by Alfred R. Waud from Harper's Weekly, November 16, 1867; p. 111, b&w film negative, Library of Congress; p. 133, photo by Ezra Stoller for Fortune, 1955, via process-vision.tumblr.com; p. 146, photo courtesy of Montgomery County, AL Sheriff's Department; p. 161, DoD photo by Master Sgt. Cecilio Ricardo, U.S. Air Force/ Released; p. 167, Bill Mauldin, The Sun-Times (Chicago); p. 169, photo by Warren K. Leffler, January 19, 1968, Library of Congress;

Documents:

p. 32, Thomas Fessenden, and p. 34, Ensign Jeremy Lister, source: Peter Bennett, *What Happened on Lexington Green*, Menlo Park: Addison-Wesley Publishing Company, 1970; p. 34, (Document 3), John R. Alden, *The American Revolution, 1775–1783*, source: New York, Harper, 1954; (Document 4), John Dickinson, *Letters from a Farmer in Pennsylvania, 1767*, source: Ashbrook Center Web site; p. 43, excerpt from *The Dominion of War*, by Fred Anderson and Andrew Cayton, Atlantic, 2005; p. 44, excerpt from T*he Seven Years War*, by Francis Parkman, Harper, 1968; p. 62, Robinson, source: *Sources in American History*, Orlando: Harcourt Brace Jovanovich, 1986; p. 88, adapted from John Hope Franklin, *Reconstruction after the Civil War*, University of Chicago Press, Copyright, 1961; p. 105, excerpt from George Plunkitt, "How I Got Rich by Honest Graft" found in *Plunkitt of Tammany Hall: A Series of Very Plain Talks on Very Practical Politics*, pp. 3–8, edited by William L. Riordan, published by Alfred A. Knopf, 1948; p. 117, excerpt from Walter LaFeber, *The New Empire: An Interpretation of American Expansion, 1860–1898*, Cornell University Press, 1963; p. 117, excerpt from Julius W. Pratt, *The Expansionists of 1898: The Acquisition of Hawaii and the Spanish Islands*, Johns Hopkins Press, 1936; reprinted Chicago,

1964; p. 119, excerpt from John Whiteclay Chambers II, *Tyranny of Change: America in the Progressive Era, 1890–1920*, New York, 1992; p. 119, excerpt from Gabriel Kolko, *The Triumph of Conservatism: A Reinterpretation of American History, 1900–1916*, New York, 1963, courtesy of Simon & Schuster; p. 148, excerpt from James Peck, *Freedom Ride*, New York: Simon & Schuster, 1962; p. 148, excerpt from Martin Luther King, Jr., "Letter from a Birmingham Jail," source: African-Studies Center – University of Pennsylvania (www.africa.upenn. edu/Articles_Gen/Letter_Birmingham.html); p. 169, excerpt from *I Have a Dream: Writings and Speeches that Changed the World*, by Martin Luther King, edited by James M. Washington, Harper San Francisco, 1992; p. 171, excerpt from *DO IT!: Scenarios of the Revolution*, by Jerry Rubin, Simon & Schuster, 1970; all others, source: Bernard Federer, *Viewpoints: USA*, New York: American Book Company, 1967.

Cover Graphic:

(left to right) photograph by Edward S. Curtis, "Shows As He Goes - half-length portrait, c. 1905," Library of Congress; map of Gettysburg battlefied, Western Maryland Railroad Company, c. 1910, Library of Congress; photograph by Lewis Wickes Hine, "Messenger boy working for Mackay Telegraph Company, Waco, Texas," September 1913, Library of Congress; photograph by Edward S. Curtis, "Chief Joseph of the Nez Perce," c. 1903, Library of Congress; cartoon by Clifford Berryman for the Washington Star, April 28, 1907, Library of Congress; illustration by Louis Dalrymple, "A Sad Case," for Puck Magazine, 1900, Library of Congress; photograph by Warren K. Leffler, "Anti-Vietnam war protest and demonstration in front of the White House in support of singer Eartha Kitt," Washington, D.C., January 19, 1968, Library of Congress; cartoon by Charles Lewis Bartholomew for the Minneapolis Journal, April 27, 1907, Library of Congress; map by Emmor B. Cope & Edgar M. Hewitt, "Gettysburg Battlefield," 1863, Library of Congress.

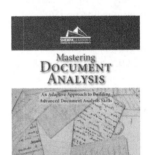

Made in United States
Orlando, FL
04 April 2024